AMERICA IN THE EYES OF THE GERMANS

America in the Eyes of the Germans

An Essay on Anti-Americanism

DAN DINER

Translated from German by Allison Brown

Introduction by Sander L. Gilman

 Markus Wiener Publishers
Princeton

THE TRANSLATION OF THEIS BOOK INTO ENGLISH WAS SUPPORTED
BY A GRANT FROM INTERNATIONES, BONN.

FOR INFORMATION WRITE TO: MARKUS WIENER PUBLISHERS
114 JEFFERSON ROAD, PRINCETON, NJ 08540

COVER DESIGN BY CHERYL MIRKIN
THIS BOOK HAS BEEN COMPOSED IN PALATINO BY CMF GRAPHIC DESIGN

LIBRARY OF CONGRESS CATALOGING-IN-PUBLICATION DATA
DINER, DAN, 1946-
[VERKEHRTE WELTEN. ENGLISH]
AMERICA IN THE EYES OF THE GERMANS:
AN ESSAY ON ANTI-AMERICANISM/DAN DINER;
INTRODUCTION BY SANDER L. GILMAN.
INCLUDES BIBLIOGRAPHICAL REFERENCES AND INDEX.
ISBN 1-55876-104-7 (HC)   ISBN 1-55876-105-5 (PB)
1. UNITED STATES—FOREIGN PUBLIC OPINION, GERMAN.
2. ANTI-AMERICANISM—GERMANY.   I. TITLE.
E183.8.G3D5513   1996
973—DC20   96-11523   CIP

MARKUS WIENER PUBLISHERS BOOKS ARE PRINTED IN THE
UNITED STATES OF AMERICA ON ACID-FREE PAPER,
AND MEET THE GUIDELINES FOR PERMANENCE AND DURABILITY
OF THE COMMITTEE ON PRODUCTION GUIDELINES FOR BOOK
LONGEVITY OF THE COUNCIL ON LIBRARY RESOURCES.

Contents

Preface

"The failure of Germans—and others—to understand Anglo-Saxon traditions and American reality is an old story."
—Hannah Arendt*

In German political rhetoric, legitimate criticisms of American actions or policies are often dismissed as anti-American prejudice. The indictment of anti-Americanism is generally put forward—so it seems—to frustrate any justified opposition to United States policies and the negative aspects of the American way of life, and thus to stigmatize the critics as distorting reality for ideological reasons.

This interpretation may often be correct. Beyond the growing frequency of charges of anti-Americanism, however, there is certainly a real problem, i.e., the phenomenon of projecting responsibility for collective evil onto the United States. Such a projection is epidemic, and it is noticeably different in nature from the accusations of "un-Americanness" put forward in the heat of fierce anti-Communism in the United States in the late 1940s and early 1950s.

This essay will deal with biased foreign perceptions of America, in particular its German form and specificities. In sum, this essay on anti-Americanism in Germany is an attempt to deal not with a phenomenon of mere prejudice,

* Letter of Hannah Arendt to the Merkur following the publication of *Politik und Verbrechen* (Politics and Crime) by Hans Magnus Enzensberger, Frankfurt 1964, reprinted in the Merkur April 1965, pp. 380-385.

but with deep-seated and long-lasting ideas, images, and metaphors that assume the character of a comprehensive interpretation.

It must be stressed that ideologically motivated anti-Americanism assuredly does not exist exclusively in Germany. It is a universal phenomenon with independent European roots. Anti-Americanism is by no means an exclusively German invention, nor is it specific to Germany. Moreover, prevailing political attitudes toward America are quite diverse within the realm of German history and political culture. Pronounced anti-Americanism coexists with uncritical philo-Americanism, curiosity along with downright indifference.

Although German attitudes toward the United States come in many varieties, a slight but perceptible negative basic attitude can be identified, which at times gains the upper hand in Germany, especially in periods of crisis and upheaval. To this attitude, to its latency and its virulence, this essay is dedicated. Admittedly, this essay is far from a study of German-American relations, even though their ups and downs may help determine the specificity, form, and various manifestations of resentment toward the United States. This study in German anti-Americanism does not intend to place blame, nor to find answers to all issues of German political culture. Rather, it aims to enlighten by means of a polemical approach.

Despite its polemics, this essay is born of a discourse with a long tradition. The material chosen is decidedly unbiased. To a German audience, the selection of examples is entirely representative for the phenomenon of historically durable prejudicial images of America. This does not mean Germans will like the image of themselves reflected in these examples. But such mortifications are part and parcel of any critique—in Germany and beyond.

This essay on anti-Americanism was first published in

German in 1993. The author's motives are wholly transparent: the book was triggered by the reactions of the German public to American involvement in the Gulf War of 1991. It became quite clear at the time that the images and resentments of anti-Americanism expressed in the period of radical transition from the order of the Cold War to a new, unknown world, had not sprung up spontaneously after a brief gestation. Now, when European history has become a bloodied rerun of its past, feelings toward the United States are much less negative, but they remain ambivalent. Old ghosts never die.

There are many to thank for this essay, above all those involved in American studies in Germany. For decades scholars have produced excellent studies regarding the image of America. This study profited greatly from their findings, especially since I have little expertise of my own in this field. However, I take full responsibility for any and all errors stemming from my ignorance. My thanks also go to colleagues, including Professor Gesine Schwan (Berlin) and Dr. Siegfried Gehrmann (Essen), who deal with the subject "America" much more professionally than I and provided important bibliographic references. I would also like to thank Karin Dietrich, who helped me survey the materials, a service made possible through the research pool of the University of Essen. Thanks are also due the editor of the German edition, Albert Sellner, for the idea of writing this essay and for taking the initiative in pushing me to elaborate on a subject that is moving to him and many others. Professors Frederick Lubich of Rutgers University and especially Bernard Lewis of Princeton University deserve thanks for helping with illustrations for this book and Dr. Inge Neske of the Bayerische Staatsbibliothek München provided additional bibliographical references. I owe a special debt of gratitude to Allison Brown for her excellent translation and the editorial effort she invested in the English-language edition. And last but not least, thanks to Markus Wiener, who spared no effort in presenting this essay to an American audience.

Tel Aviv/ Essen
January 1996

Introduction

Sander L. Gilman

Goliath Armstrong: The typical
America Western movie scene.
Lustige Blätter, 1921

American Humor: America is the freest country in the world.
Simplicissimus, 1922

"I would really like to marry in America, but not marry an American. Or maybe I'll marry an American and we'll live on the Riviera. A villa on the Riviera. Marble steps down to the water. Lying naked on the marble." Thus does Arthur Schnitzler's eponymous Fräulein Else, the young Jewish girl about to be given to her father's debtor, imagine the most perfect of marriages. America without the Americans; the Americans in Europe—this is the mirror-image of Henry James' Daisy Miller—a dream of America as formed in Vienna in the 1920s. America as the empty land—empty of the quarrels of the past, of Europe, of culture, of love; but the Americans—always rich and naive and sexy—accessible and acceptable relocated in the Europe of the Viennese fantasy.

Dan Diner's insightful study of the Germans' imaginary America is powerful, and in Germany it cut much too close to the bone. This book provides a permanent outsider's narrative of the love/hate relationship between the Germans and their "America." Dan Diner, a professor in Germany as well as Israel (and regular visitor to my "America"), spins his tale with elegance and insight. The Americanization of Germany seems like a problem of the post-Shoah world and yet Diner demonstrates how deep the fantasy of America lies in German consciousness.

It is primarily Germany, German history, and German texts that Dan Diner examines, yet the Austrian fantasy of America is part of a German-language construction of America as the locus of the Other. It can be a positive Other—America as the space where the non-European world permits the freedom of the German from the social, moral, and intellectual constraints of "Germany," before and after its actual political creation in 1871; it can be the negative Other—America as the topography of corruption and decay, where only the unfit live. It is no accident that Dan Diner, from his own outsider position, understands this split image of the construction of America as analogous to the German construction of the "Jew." Diner's image of the American as the Jew and the Jew as the American points out the continuities within the world of stereotypical representations. Indeed, one can even mention that the psychiatric literature of the fin de siècle had a nosological category called "Americanization," a illness of modern life which was manifest most often among European Jews. The Jews suffer from the same inability to cope with the pressures of modern life as do the Americans. The difference is that the pathological Americans are "rootless" in a specific space; the ill Jews have no space in which they can be rooted.

Dan Diner's map of the German topography of difference, however, can have an equivalent space for the Jews only after the founding of the State of Israel. Indeed, the Gulf War showed how anti-Americanism in Germany and especially anti-Jewish resentment in the peace movement and among its fellow-travellers saw the war as an American/Jewish/Israeli invasion. The virulent shouts that it was ISRAEL that was causing the Gulf War, rather than Iraqi expansionism, simply echoed the cries against American imperial hegemony that carried on the anti-Semitic associations of Jew and American from the nineteenth century.

But what about the topography of Otherness in German culture prior to 1948/49 What function does America serve in the culture of Germany in the late nineteenth and early twentieth century? Let me make a specific proposal to continue Dan Diner's insightful and often frightening account. The image of America, especially in the world of Karl Bodmer, the Swiss artist of the Plains Indians, or Charles Sealsfield, the Austrian novelist of the American West, or even later in the works of Karl May (who never visited America), provided a model for understanding the role of the German in the German claim for colonies in Africa. How does the German exist as a German in strange climes, with strange people; does the German collapse into identification with the "New World," or does the German keep his own sense of his difference (and superiority)? If the American/Jew in Europe is the "race out of its appropriate space" and therefore ill and dangerous, how does the German in Africa avoid this fate?

By the time Karl May wrote his "Africa" novels to accompany his Old Shatterhand novels of the American West, these parallels were simply assumed. America was Africa and Africa, America. The German, who often collapses in the German colonial fiction of the 1890s by into "going native" or sickening and dying, is patterned after the figures in fictions who are "tired of America" and its coarseness. The rehearsal for the construction of "Africa" in the age of German colonial expansion is the idea of America in German consciousness in the nineteenth century. It is a place of testing where universal (read: German) values of separateness and sense of self preserve the "white man" in the wilderness.

The German "experience" of America, from the stranding of German immigrants in Lousiana during the Mississippi Bubble to the end of the nineteenth century, was filtered through German literary models. It was received and was formed by the demands of a German process of German self-identification in the world of literature—for culture came to be the space for the German trying to understand the world. Here the tie to the Jew might also be made. For Jewish culture in the Diaspora is lived culture mirrored and focused through texts—the People of the Book lived in books. The missing topography comes to be the place where each constructs the Other.

After 1871, however, real places come to define reality. I have a land and you don't! says the German to the Jew. But after 1948, it is the Jew who can gesture towards Israel and say: this is my land; and your land, Germany, is scarred by its divisions, by the Wall, as a brand of shame. America, and the Americans, came to represent that inarticulate shame of the divided map. "I am a Berliner," John Kennedy shouted into the wind—was he really? Certainly not. He was American, the occupying power. For the Germans there was no fantasy of "liberation" such as that held in Vienna. (It was only the then-German President Richard von Weizsacker who could evoke this fifty years after the end of the war—when Germany was again united and intact, with no scars of the past marking her topography.)

West German anti-Americanism after 1945 was not related to Joe McCarthy's charges of un-Americanism against the liberals of his day. It was a recycling of the inner anxieties of what it meant to be a German. East German anti-Americanism was of a purer kind—it was the Cold War writ large. And yet even in the "New Federal States" (the old GDR) the American came to have meaningful symbolic value in a system of constructing the feared and the desired.

The Germans, perhaps more than any other European "nation," have been forced to use America as a means of representing their own self-understanding in the most complex manner. For the sense of quadruple loss in the twentieth century for German identity is extraordinary. First the loss of the Imperial German identity, so prized by

Catholic, Protestant and Jew in Germany, at least after the fin de siècle. This identity was lost, destroyed, mangled in the killing fields of Belgium and France; then the Republican identity, skin deep for most, but prized by many; then the Nazi identity, accepted by most, internalized by all; then the socialist identity of the GDR, prized by few, accepted by most. How many Germanys have there been on the topography?—as many as the multiple states of Germany before 1871.—How has the Bavarian and the Thuringian become Imperial, Republican, Nazi, Capitalist and Communist?—what are their enemies, who are they not, who were they not? "America" functioned in the symbolic language of defining the self in all of these permutations. For the discourse of difference that Dan Diner sketches in this remarkable book is the discourse of who the Germans believe themselves not to be: When America is good, it is because German self-representation is bad; when America is bad, it defines the positive nature of the fantasy of the German. The disequilibrium here is evident— "America" (and not the American) defines the German (and not "Germany"). Here the anxiety of individual versus group identity is played out in a system of symbolic representations.

Diner's book is more than merely a sketch of the "image of America": it is a measure of what the Germans (however defined) imagine America to be. I am reminded of my university years in Germany in the early 1960s. When I was introduced to members of my father's generation and was recognized by my accent and clothing as an "Ami" (an American), the discussion of the past took a remarkable turn—suddenly no one had fought on the Western front, everyone had fought against "our" common enemy (in 1961), the Communists; when I was understood to be a Jew (as I was involved in Jewish student groups), suddenly no one had ever been in the Wehrmacht on the East-

ern front, in the killing field of Russia. This was not du-
plicitousness. It was a sign that we imagine ourselves into
the world and are constantly reimagining ourselves. We
are the collection not of our experiences, but of our fantasies about those experiences. Dan Diner's book presents
a case study for this in a clear and admirable manner.
Enjoy!

Sander L. Gilman
The University of Chicago
February 1996

Reversals

MIRRORING AMERICA

Meeting of Europeans and the New World Natives
Cosmographia, 1550

Freedom in Dollarland
Simplicissimus, 1910

"In the beginning, all the world was America." That, in any case, is how John Locke characterized the significance of the continent in 1690 in his *Two Treatises of Civil Government*.[1] There is a trace of the story of creation in such a formulation. The words of Spanish historian Francisco Lopez de Gomara, a contemporary of Locke, reflect the same force of a founding act. As early as 1552, he saw the discovery of America as the greatest event since the creation of the world, except for the "incarnation and death of Him who created it," of course, as he piously qualified his statement.[2] And then in 1776, the historic year of the American Revolution, Adam Smith assessed the "discovery of America" as one of "the two greatest and most important events recorded in the history of mankind."[3] The impact of discovering America was indeed far-reaching, both for its physical realities and for human consciousness. The consequences of the event have remained linked to questions of faith, albeit those of a more profane nature, to this day.

The debate concerning America gained momentum, especially after the Declaration of Independence. There was mention of a "second discovery" of the continent, and relevant opinions were legion, ranging from paeans to profound condemnation. In a letter of 1778, economist Anne Robert Jacques Turgot expressed enthusiasm that America represented something like "the hope of humanity"; in any case, it was a shining example for Europe.[4] In his *Recherches philosophiques sur les Americains*, published in 1768/69 in Berlin, on the other hand, Cornelius de Pauw complained that the discovery and conquest of the New

World was "the greatest tragedy" ever to befall humanity.[5] America continues to keep Europe's imagination in suspense as no other continent has.[6] Unlike Asia and Africa, America was a product of European imaginations from the very beginning. According to John H. Elliott, as a result of this projection, "America and Europe were for ever inseparable, their destinies interlocked."[7]

So the discovery of America resembled a founding act. The world appeared to be created anew from that moment on, to the extent that it had to be rethought. John Locke's statement can be understood in this way; it describes both an unspoiled pristine state and a new, internal chronology in history. "In the beginning, all the world was America" clearly denotes the primordial state as a wilderness— everything that lies beyond the blessings of civilization emanating from the human spirit and created by human hands. The task of extending and completing the Old World has been confidently incorporated into this diagnosis: America should become Europe. But this is merely one possible interpretation.

There is yet another way of reading "In the beginning, all the world was America"—especially today, when having experienced all forms of disappointment and weariness of progress. Unscathed by culture, the "New World" means the original state in the sense of a paradise lost, a utopia relocated to prehistoric times, beyond the civilizing fall from grace that is modernity. Such an idea of paradise is nothing particularly new.

The imagined locations of earlier concepts of salvation in a world without conflict had already shifted westward. This was the case of Thomas More's *Utopia* of 1516, as well as Francis Bacon's *New Atlantis*, published in 1627.[8] Against the backdrop of disappointing conditions in the Old World, it was easier to imagine Arcadia and Eden on the far side of the Atlantic. The Humanists, at least, tended to project their dreams onto the New World. "Here were a people who. . . seem to lyve in the goulden worlde of the which owlde wryters speake so much: wherin men lyved simplye and innocentlye without inforcement of lawes, without quarerelling Iudges and libelles, contente onely to satisfie nature, without further vexation for knowlege of thinges to come."[9]

To Europeans, America meant the primordial and natural state in two senses. First, untamed nature, which Europeans of the time thought could be redeemed by the spread of Christianity and civilization. And second, innocent nature, a longed-for paradise spoiled by that very civilization that has since been named "America" and—today—is condemned as the epitome of modernity and corrupter of the world. These two versions of America have one thing in common: America remains the counterworld to Europe, a complementary continent of occidental civilization and a screen upon which to project all the images and metaphors arising from its contrast to Europe; a screen upon which to project isolated portions of self-hate owing mainly to modernity, but blamed only on the New World.[10] America carries the stigma of a civilization that spans the globe.

The discourse surrounding commemoration of the 500th anniversary of the discovery of America carried obvious aspects of such an association. As if the discovery and settling of America represented humanity's original sin, the rhetoric almost unanimously suggested the universal fall from grace of world history, a type of founding act of evil. Looking closely and listening, it even appears that this incriminating act of discovery originated not on the Iberian peninsula of Europe, but on the North American continent. In any case, contemporary views have propagated such an impression—not only in Latin America, where Creoles and other descendants of Hispanic con-

quistadors, strangely enough, have traditionally vented
hostility toward America whenever the United States is
mentioned.

It is the United States that bears the stigma of America.
The suffering caused by human hands in the New World
and elsewhere is blamed first and foremost on the United
States. And it is the United States that is held accountable
for the seemingly unbounded expansion of bourgeois
society. To the United States and only to the United States,
a lifestyle is attributed that completely levels out any cultural diversity. The universally bewailed loss of familiar
surroundings and traditional certainties know only one
cause—the United States, that omnipresent place, that
Moloch of the modern age that aims to conquer the world.
Ludwig Marcuse complained in the 1950s that America
was the ideal scapegoat for the general process of alienation for the simple reason that "it is everywhere." The
universality of ways of life associated with the United
States makes it "everyone's more powerful, too visible
neighbor," as it were.[11] Ignazio Silone is also of the opinion
that "America is everywhere."[12] Relative to European
dimensions, the United States really does seem gigantic.
An American shipping company has emphasized the
paradoxical mental impact of the comparison in their
advertising slogan: "The world is small, yet America is
great."[13]

The origins of the hostility toward America are varied.
One significant aspect of an aversion that is gradually
becoming a worldview is the developing contrast between
Europe and America. To a certain extent, America is considered Europe's alter ego. Both the historical separation
and the political coming together of America and Europe
have had a traumatic impact at times. The mere circumstances that turned Europeans into Americans are proof of
this. The annual rings of European crises can be read by

the waves of immigration to the United States. And layers
of American memories—which have little good to say
about Europe—are in turn deposited on these crises.
American freedom was after all a reaction to the lack of
liberties in Europe. That was why Thomas Jefferson
wished for "an ocean of fire" between the two continents.

The European consciousness that dissociated itself
from America saw the New World as a hotbed of threats to
its own's values. Decay and decadence seemed to emanate
from it and increasingly spread to Europe, much to the
horror of a certain public.

At the time of the Enlightenment, such fantastic images were directed mostly at natural phenomena. Without
ever having set eyes on the New World, the highly respected scholar Comte de Buffon confidently propagated
the attitude that physiologically and psychologically
degenerate forms of life existed in America. Everyone and
everything degenerated: Settlers, farm animals, and pets
brought over from Europe, supposedly showed considerable signs of degeneration after a period of time. The
physical appearance of Native Americans was taken as
a basis, as they had little body hair in comparison with
Europeans.[14] Even the above-mentioned Abbé de Pauw
considered the living conditions awaiting Europeans in
the New World to be life-threatening, or in any case un-
bearable. Aside from degenerative phenomena that triggered fear and loathing, such as animals without tails,
dogs that had lost their barks, and people with square-
shaped heads, the environment was supposedly poisoned
by worms, snakes, reptiles, and insects.[15]

In the post-Enlightenment period, metaphors based on
natural images gradually disappeared from interpretions
and evaluations of the New World. In their place, images
started concentrating on social phenomena that differed so
greatly from those in Europe.[16] The motif of degeneration

persisted in this area as well, though in a political sense. The feared decline was henceforth based on the idea and reality of equality and freedom. Conversely, friends of the New World were enthused about the idea of the republic, of freedom and equality as they were realized in America. The two attitudes had something in common; that is, they saw America as Europe's future, and thus the contours of the future *per se.* In a negative sense, their own fears of decline were reflected in "America."

It was not Oswald Spengler, but the bestselling author Moeller van den Bruck—who coined the term "The Third Reich"—who was also the first to say that the rise of America represented the complementary process to the "decline of the West."[17] And it is no coincidence that in 1932 Aldous Huxley's oppressive, modernistic vision of doom included the "New World" in its title like a stigma. In the European consciousness, "America" was a metaphor for those images illustrating primarily the darker side of modernity.

Alexis de Tocqueville's actual intention in traveling through and studying North America was to catch a glimpse of the future of humanity. In his classical work *Democracy in America,* he conceded that he was less interested in America itself than in examining the democratic way of life *per se.*[18] This was confirmed in a letter he wrote to John Stuart Mill: "America was only my framework, *démocratie* was the subject."[19] The advantages and disadvantages of America were a subject of his curiosity insofar as he felt the New World anticipated the future of Europe.

What de Tocqueville discovered in the United States in 1835 annoyed Europeans no end—namely, the polity as pure society, wholly without a state. This was indeed a reversal of European experience, in which the state of the early modern age was a prerequisite to order and prosperity. America, on the other hand, underwent a totally op-

posite development. From the very beginning, it was con-
ceived as a society pure, definitely lacking state. And from
the very beginning, freedom-obsessed Americans showed
little appreciation of the very institution that inspired
Europe's historical consciousness and was celebrated by
Hegel as the incarnation of cultural superiority.

The philosopher of German Idealism believed America
was condemned to be merely a "bourgeois society." This
was definitely linked to a value judgment in terms of historical development—that is, America's inferiority. Hegel
felt that North America could only be compared with
Europe at all if "the members of the political body [civil
society] shall have begun to be pressed back on each other.
. . . It is for America to abandon the ground on which hith-
erto the History of the World has developed itself. What
has taken place in the New World up to the present time is
only an echo of the Old World—the expression of a foreign
Life; and as a Land of the Future, it has no interest for us
here. . . ."[20]

Contemporary critic Manfred Henningsen related the
paradoxical connection between overall nature and failure
to appreciate the United States, on the one hand, to concealed aspects of European consciousness with a Eurocentric philosophy of history, on the other. This had to do
with traces of Hegelian thought or with historical thought
in the Hegelian tradition. In his view, even the fact that the
French Revolution was always preferred to the American
one revealed a Hegelian undertone. Despite the Declaration of Human Rights in the New World that preceded the
French Revolution, with its major emphasis on liberty, for
over two hundred years it has always led a shadowy existence hardly befitting it. "The 'rising of the sun' in France
led to a total eclipse of America."[21]

In Henningsen's opinion, the understanding and course
of history in Europe has been interpreted solely in terms of

images and concepts of the French Revolution, both positive and negative. The German public's interest in the
United States already started to wane with the convening
of the Etats Generaux in France.[22] From the very start of
the Great Revolution, the United States as a political phenomenon was seen through the prism of French events.
And since, due to its colonial origins, it eluded all the concepts that had been constitutive for Continental Europe, it
was largely ignored, or even viewed as fundamentally
hostile. Meanwhile, the pattern of the French Revolution,
and the understanding of history resulting from it, became
increasingly universalized.

The extreme significance granted the French Revolution at the expense of its American predecessor—especially because of its delayed, "catch-up" effect in the
colonial regions outside Europe—is mainly because of the
October Revolution. The latter was not interpreted as a
continuation of the ideas of 1789.[23] Both in terms of the
philosophy of history and political semantics, the October
Revolution was scorned as the executor of its great predecessor; the French Revolution and the October Revolution
were seen as the unequal twins of universal emancipation.
The controversy over the impact and significance of the
French Revolution was carried out using the pros and
cons of the Russian October. After the Bolshevik coup
d'état, anyone who expressed support for the events of
1789 was implicitly considered a supporter of 1917—and
vice versa. This intrinsic connection between the two revolutions in twentieth century contemporary consciousness
leads, after the historical end without a conclusion of one
of them—the Russian Revolution—to the end of the historical impact of the other—the French Revolution. Historian François Furet thus came to the conclusion that the
secular collapse of "real socialism" brought not only an
annulment of the historical significance of the October

events; with it, the historical impact of the French Revolution had also come to an end.

It is not that the values of the Great Revolution were thereby destroyed. On the contrary, the decline of communism gave them yet another prod toward fulfillment. In that light, the values of the French Revolution prevailed over those of the Russian. According to a teleological understanding of history that presupposes a succession of revolutions leading towards an ultimate utopian state, universal interpretations that linked the French and Russian Revolutions might very well have exhausted their usefulness with the end of communism.

The impact of American principles, emerging in a stronger form universally, can only be understood against the backdrop of a reality that has fallen apart and the worldview that went with it, represented by the counterpart of "real socialism." This only refers to principles and values associated with the United States throughout its history, not with the real and less pleasant problems of the virtual United States. But the principles of the American Revolution, promoted historically by the United States, have a global impact irrespective of that. When students in a despotic state erect a replica of the Statue of Liberty as a symbol of their demands, it is the principles of 1776 that are meant, the democratic ethos for which the United States of America stands, above and beyond its actual, empirical constitution. A paradoxical picture emerges: in 1989—two hundred years after the French Revolution and, at the same time, the collapse of the aftermath of the Red October—the year 1776 stepped out of the Eurocentric shadow of 1789, a shadow that had grown through the blinding effects of the year 1917.

How the relationship to America might shift, now that communism has declined along with the related remnants of a Hegelian interpretation of history, is a question of the future, like it or not. A change in attitudes toward America is unfathomable if one does not critically acknowledge ideological hostility toward America—that is, anti-Americanism. This is all the more necessary since the United States has started focussing more on domestic concerns since the end of bi-polarity and the east-west conflict. It probably would not be very good for Europe if the United States were to bid the old continent a final farewell. The experience of the period between the two world wars bodes no good. And European unification efforts, which had been the focus of so much hope, are proving—at the peak in integration achieved thus far—to be far more arduous than was expected and are by no means irreversible, a definite cause for concern. All of this is happening in the face of tempestuous thrusts of nationalism and ethnification surging from the realm of the former Eastern bloc—that is, historically central, eastern, and south-eastern European region.

Portraying the traditions and effects of hostile attitudes toward America is by no means unproblematic. After all, not all perceptions are products of irrational spouting of blind figments of the imagination. It is all the more difficult since ideological prejudice tends to fix upon real phenomena. The closeness of these negative feelings to reality might confuse an observer, insofar as a prejudice might in fact contain "a seed of truth"—a distorted truth eagerly taken up and shown off like a trophy.

The difficulty in separating aversion to America from true-to-life renderings of experienced reality involves a problem with the presentation. In individual cases, it is virtually impossible to sufficiently distinguish exaggerated projections from real phenomena. It is often difficult to separate anti-American metaphors as an expression of ideology and hostility, on the one hand, and as a critique of excesses in the United States that are truly worthy of criticism, of problems in the political culture, of social structures and economic conduct, on the other. The respective justifications are nevertheless worlds apart. Typical of anti-Americanism are complaints of lost values and traditions. The European variety has always distinguished itself by an aggressive sentimentality over the loss of a mostly class-related framework that melts away in the sunlight of democratic and republican values. Such laments were, incidentally, by no means expressed only by true members of the aristocracy. Even the middle class found itself increasingly guided by ethics opposed to ideas of equality. Objections to this on ideological grounds are usually directed at the breakdown of class boundaries, for which America stands.

The writing on America by one Leo L. Matthias can be introduced here as both an example and a prototype. They would have been worthy of no further notice, had they not served in the 1950s and 1960s as a downright arsenal of anti-Americanism used as ammunition by all sorts of eager epigones. Their topoi can be traced to particular works by successful German authors, and they enjoy a lasting renaissance through constant repetition.

Matthias's method is obvious. He lied by using the truth. His observations might be accurate and well-documented in isolation. But the generalizations based on selective perception and the resulting findings totally miss the point; they prove to be invented ideological misstatements. His *Entdeckung Amerikas Anno 1953* (Discovery of America in the Year 1953)[24] and his book that appeared a good decade later, *Die Kehrseite der USA* (The Other Side of the USA),[25] are true catechisms of anti-Americanism. They include excellent examples of archetypal expressions of an ideological stereotype.

Matthias's anti-American travel writing reads like the protest of a dying way of life against the victorious grave-

diggers to whom the unspeakable future belongs. Liberty
and equality were subsumed beneath status and class—
America versus Europe. According to Matthias, while the
ultimate social principle in Europe was merit rather than
profit, in the United States the cold-hearted rules of a
profit-oriented society prevailed.[26] Teachers, scholars,
judges, and government officials thus suffered an irreversible loss of authority; in his view, subservient social
classes and preexisting traditional differences in social status were in the process of dissolution. Matthias felt that
the labor movement even was lacking the notion of a
working class. Of course, it also lacked any class consciousness.[27] The same went for work itself. Since it was
nothing more than a "job," the activity had no emotional
content and degenerated to mere function. In contrast,
European society was shown in a positive light, in which
social standing and class continued to have their traditional influence. Matthias expressed in all seriousness the
opinion that in Europe, even a domestic servant was not
motivated by wages alone; her work contributed to the
"peace and quiet of the head of the house," the "happiness
of the lady of the house," and the "cheerfulness of the
children." In America, on the other hand, he believed
pride never centered on the work itself, but on wages
alone.[28]

Matthias argued that the lack of social standing and
status in American society had been accompanied by analogous developments in ethics, morality, and religion.
Although even Matthias saw the United States as a very
religious society, he found that its religion differed consid-
erably from its European equivalent. "Christianity in
America has become pseudo-Christianity. The only thing
it shares with European Christianity is the name and a few
liturgical rituals; and it is questionable if its doctrine
should even still be regarded as religious at all."[29] The

author considered the primary reason for the lack of true religiosity to be Protestant sectarianism, but even more so the lack of true Catholicism, the denomination still characterized by hierarchy and standing. No true faith can exist where status has given way to sheer striving for profit. "American society had to become areligious for the same reasons that it has become 'classless.'" In order to survive, even American Catholicism had to sacrifice its soul. "It had to assume the character of a Protestant sect."[30]

The emotional aspect of openly expressed disdain for American Protestantism, especially the almost literal railing of Puritanism and Calvinism as the epitome of hypocrisy and sanctimoniousness, goes hand in hand with a consistent display of sympathy for Catholic Latin America. There, European ways of life prevailed, in contrast to the North with its strong Anglo-Saxon influence. These sympathies evidenced an old European idiosyncrasy whose roots go deeper than everyday anti-Americanism.

America is considered the only civilized Western country with neither Catholicism nor nobility to call its own.[31] It is thus a land without "authority in the traditional sense."[32] An additional element of classical anti-Americanism follows in the wake of such statements. The constant ridicule of Americans as having lost their military competence and soldierly virtues is in keeping with the notion that a true army is simply incompatible with unrestricted democracy.[33] The idea that Americans possess no military qualities whatsoever is a standing claim of classical anti-Americanism. It has extended through two world wars and can be observed to this day. For example, during the 1991 Gulf War, the United States was widely criticized as militarily incompetent, with controlled aggression masked as pacifism: fire power rather than fighting spirit.

In addition, Matthias, in true aristocratic style, showed his disapproval of the American disdain of the military by pointing out that in the United States, no girl would be proud "to be seeing a soldier."[34]

Such attitudes are generally connected with open support for the aristocratic southern lifestyle that was wiped out during the Civil War by massing of mere material by the democratic North and its industrialism. Matthias, with his orientation toward traditional values, even showed a certain understanding for slavery. He did not approve of the classification of Blacks as Negroes; on the contrary, this deplorable situation is offered as proof of the hypocritical character of America's "freedom." But he shows understanding for more comfortable forms of paternalistic rule under which Blacks, in some instances, felt secure and safe. Despite all injustices, he believed the slaves still tended to feel self-esteem and pride, and could "attain a certain social status in the Southern social order."[35]

Complaints about loss of tradition of course also include paternalistic concerns over the status of women and the shift in women's role that began in the United States. In the anti-American attitudes of the 1920s, in particular, alarm prevailed with respect to the social power of women in the United States and the related loss of status for men. U.S. society, according to Matthias, was all but maternalistic. Everywhere, a horror of the woman as an authority figure could be glimpsed. "The power of the American woman is thus the most monstrous form of woman's power that history has known."[36] And if that did not suffice, this unpleasant finding was supplemented by the complaint that women in America paid for their apparent equality with the loss of their former femininity. "The femaleness of women has disappeared in America," conjectured Matthias.[37] This referred to the courtly type of woman that was imagined by a bourgeois mentality. And this was sacrificed, in his opinion, to the nonhierarchical American democracy and profit-oriented society. It is small wonder that love has become impoverished in America as nowhere else.[38] Americans, he said, are totally incapable of maintaining these courtly European forms. Although American men might desire women, they do not respect them.[39] The reasons for this are obvious: "There were never handmaidens in America and there were never ladies-in-waiting.[40] In America, everything had disappeared that was necessary for emotional life—"the tragedy, the social status, and even the love."[41] Just as gender roles in America are shorn of all authenticity and love, Americans have been condemned to sterility in other areas requiring creativity as well. If they were declared devoid of all military virtues, this was even more true for higher level abilities requiring a combination of technical and military capabilities—attributes that appear to have been inherited by the bourgeois and aristocratic nations of Europe. It is disclosed to readers who accept this argument that America "had state-of-the-art war technology neither in the First nor the Second World War."[42] No wonder: War technology could not "reach a higher level than technology in general, and technology could not surpass the general level of education."[43] It apparently went without saying that education in the United States is not the best. Supposedly, the USA was outstanding in neither aircraft nor tank construction during World War II. Quite the contrary, it was outdone by other countries in all relevant areas of war technology. As examples, Matthias mentioned the German "Königstiger" tank, introduced during the final phase of the war, and the Soviet MIG-15 fighter plane, employed during the Korean War by the communist North.[44] The Americans, he said, had nothing substantial to compare. This was also the case in other areas that experienced relevant innovations. "Even the insecticide DDT was not an American, but a Swiss product." Matthias pays a mocking tribute to the American genius of in vention, which he considers invalid. "These statements are not meant to claim that America invented nothing during the war—the 'Jeep' will survive World War II by decades. . . ."[45]

Science and technology were supposedly not the only fields in which Americans have little but imitations to show; in the area of government as well—obviously the domain of European statecraft—its abilities were considered mediocre. "A businessman is not a statesman," said Matthias succinctly. By setting the economic versus the political, America ends up, in traditional perceptions, reduced to the utilitarian attributes of a commercial enterprise. Europe, on the other hand, could refer to the formative effect of state and nation. Anyone who did not, like Europe, have access to the classical state, and was not nourished by the political culture of a past hierarchy, would prove incapable of truly exercising power. America was thus not even seen in a position "to govern a couple of foreign islands like Puerto Rico or the Philippines. . . ."[46] America's power was bounded by the limits of the commercial, consumer character of the New World. This does not mean that the United States scorned power. On the contrary, the character of what Matthias refered to as the "violent businessman" is devoid of all ethical provisos; his sphere of action is unlimited. Business people strive toward nothing more or less than "the goal of world domination."

The European tradition is very different. It has supposedly never known the "businessman as a sovereign power." Even Genoa and Venice did not experience such direct greed for wealth, "for it was not the businesspeople who ruled there, but an aristocracy that was involved in trade." Up until 1861, the only power that could compete with the "violent businessman" who was spreading throughout the world was that of the "plantation owner and slave-holder in the South." The slavery business failed, which is why Matthias felt that in the end the American state became a plaything in the hands of selfish interest groups greedily scrapping for power and wealth. The violent businessman as a typology was insatiable. Beyond that, he supposedly appeared, confusingly enough, in various roles. "Today he is co-owner of a bank that finances war supplies; tomorrow he is the minister of defense who increases the very same supplies. Today he is the general manager of one of the largest aircraft manufacturers, and tomorrow he is a general in the air corps." His rule, according to Matthias, started at the moment he drafted a constitution that corresponded to his commercial needs. The founding of the United States was not at all honorable. It was nothing but a "financial transaction."[47]

Accordingly, the United States stands for business and the essence of abstraction—both of which are expressions of alienation. An American, characterized by Matthias as a "pure businessman," regards as secondary anything that cannot be reduced to an "economic common denominator." In this anti-abstract sense, incidentally, the "pure businessman" is related to the "pure scientist." Such distorted observations were taken up by an entire world of anti-modernistic rationalizations and simplifications. When physicists abstract from the objects they perceive, like businessmen they "consider as secondary things that are not suited to a series of number, mass, and weight. In both cases, the material world becomes impoverished through the process of abstraction. . . ."[48] In fact, that is the basic tenet of anti-American prejudice: To the blinded consciousness, America is a "paradigm of the alienating experiences of modernity."[49]

Leo L. Matthias's descriptions by no means reflect a particularly extreme genre of anti-American literature. They are quite paradigmatic in nature. The frequency with which they appear, in varying degrees of density, layering, and form, though primarily the fact that they are passed down for generations, clearly shows that anti-Americanism is a long-lasting and deep-seated ideological hostility. Like a cultural code, it is expressed even by people having neither practical nor theoretical knowledge of America.

In this way, though not only in this way, anti-Americanism resembles anti-Semitism structurally (as well as in the selection of metaphors). In some respects, anti-Americanism can even be understood as a further stage in the secularized hostility towards Jews. Even though the two phenomena, on account of their different developmental histories, could never be considered identical, they both represent ideologically shaped reactions to modernity. Anti-American and antisemitic vocabularies include strikingly synonymous images and metaphors—especially those used to denounce phenomena of the financial sphere as the root of all evil: money, interest, commerce, the stock market. The *Historisches Schlagwörterbuch* (Historical Subject Catalogue), published in 1906 by Otto Ladendorf, mentions, under the subject "Americanism," its relationship to those characteristics attributed to Jews by antisemites. It quotes a "modern documentation" with the quaint title *Was die Isar rauscht* (The Murmering Isar River), which states categorically: "The American, lacking ideals, . . . will become the person of the future even in old Europe; in a certain sense, one can now characterize the Jews as the representatives of Americanism here. Judaization [*Verjudung*] is actually Americanization."[50]

Such an organic linkage between hostility toward Americans and toward Jews could be observed for decades. Max Horkheimer characterized it as significant that "everywhere that one finds anti-Americanism, anti-Semitism is also prevalent." There are many reasons for this, not the least being the substratal impact of the recent past.

"America, irrespective of its motives, saved Europe from total enslavement. Today, the response all over, not only in Germany, has been widespread and far-reaching hostility toward America. There has been much conjecture about the origin of this—resentment, envy, but also errors made by the American government and its citizens, all play a role. . . . The general malaise caused by cultural decline seeks a scapegoat, and for the aforementioned and other reasons, they find the Americans and, in America itself, once again the Jews, who supposedly rule America."[51]

The nature of ideology accords both complexes of prejudice yet another commonality that can be characterized as a defense against self-awareness—namely, denying the existence of such phenomena. There might well be a willingness here and there to admit the existence of such patterns of prejudice at a very abstract level, but actually harboring such feelings is vehemently denied.

Defensive reactions demonstrated by the denial of anti-Americanism sometimes take on grotesque proportions. British historian E.P. Thompson, for example, introduced an article meant to be critical of America by declaring that he, of all people, could hardly be accused of anti-Americanism since he himself was half American by birth.[52]

It is quite typical for anti-Americanism to justify itself by an author's reference of his or her membership in the incriminated community. This is heavily entwined with the concept of the "other America" with which the author agrees, in complete contrast to "America pure and simple." Constant and stubborn reference to the testimony of "another America"—*contra* America—is thus at the heart of anti-American argumentation.

Such deception is rooted in the denial of one's own prejudice. Anti-Americanism as it has developed is not only a form of xenophobia directed against Americans, as ethnocentric European nationalism is primarily directed against foreigners. Americans are by no means perceived as random foreigners. In this context, instead they represent a contrast to the European self. Thus misdirected awareness of anti-Americanism is an ideologically loaded rationalization that makes it easier to come to terms with realities of life and lifestyles that have become difficult to comprehend.

Insofar, America is not simply "foreign" in the sense of a foreign community, a foreign country, and everything generally connected with the term "foreign." Rather, America is "different"—but different in the sense of a specific "other," as a separate internal entity that represents reviled aspects of civilization and thus a part of the speakers themselves. There is more than just a hint of polemic truth in the statement by Jean Baudrillard that only Europeans could recognize the truth of America.[53]

Are these reservations valid for criticism of America by America itself? Can such criticism also fall under the ideological verdict of anti-Americanism? The transition from criticism based on one's own American values to criticism in the sense of hostility toward the foundations of the American sense of itself—which is in fact in the process of becoming an ideology—is very fluid. As that is not the subject of this treatise, it shall suffice to indicate that in the United States, positions critical of America and the liberalism it represents are often confronted with sweeping accusations of ideological anti-Americanism. In particular, radically liberal, pro-Soviet, and pro-"Third World" views, no matter what their origins, have periodically been characterized politically as "un-American" (a recent U.S. study of anti-Americanism by Paul Hollander suffers from this deficiency). That sort of reductionism is not employed here.

Despite its expression within a quite unified worldview, a wide range in the degree of hostility directed against America can be observed in the European consciousness. Such predominantly cultural arrogance highlights the contrast between the organic European, and the American construct burdened with the stigma of being mere imitation. The arrogant words of Georges Clemenceau are significant in this regard; he dismissed America as "a progression from barbarism to decadence without a detour through culture." George Bernard Shaw is also called upon as a witness, having declared "the hundred percent American to be ninety-nine percent idiot."[54] In the aftermath of the Spanish-American War, the Pope felt obliged in 1899 to warn of the danger of Americanism. This might appear understandable given his interests.[55] It is more disappointing that Sigmund Freud also joined in the anti-American chorus—he, who received overwhelming praise and recognition in the United States even during his lifetime. The founder of psychoanalysis told his friend and biographer Ernest Jones his unflattering view that America represented a "gigantic mistake."[56]

This may very well be circular reasoning. By the very nature of the written form, statements on or about America are by and large provided by the educated. And it was predominantly the educated classes—middle class and intelligentsia—who made disparaging remarks about America. Such an attitude was apparently tied largely to social status. In any case, Ludwig Marcuse determined that anti-Americanism was "hardly ever found among streetcar conductors, hairdressers, maids, or chauffeurs, though it was extremely prevalent among journalists, professors, and theater people."[57] The latter generally were not eager to relinquish the security of their status. America's democratic prospects frightened them. Lower classes judged America in a different way. Victims of nineteenth century European industrialism opted for America via emigration to the New World. America presented itself to the poor and impoverished time and time again as a promised land that provided opportunities for those without means who had long since been forgotten in Europe. The fact that America offered asylum for Europeans until the 1920s should certainly not let anyone forget that historically it was also a "slaughterhouse for Native Americans" and "Africa's prison" (Henningsen). That is why there are also different perspectives with regard to the American experience. The interpretation by people in America whose ancestors were either members of the native population or brought to the New World as slaves must differ from that of those whose ancestors immigrated from Europe. Remembering the bloody sides of American history is just as necessary for the sake of historical truth as rejecting their instrumentalization for the purpose of defaming the United States. "The fact that America was not the asylum for all humanity cannot erase its significance for Europe."[58]

Although it is by no means a specifically German phenomenon, it appears that anti-American hostility lies deeper in the political mentality in Germany than elsewhere in Europe. Germany's defeats in two world wars may well be the reason. Both times it was the United States' entering the war that contributed decisively to Germany's military subjugation. Preexisting cultural animosity toward America was not insignificant in allowing such disastrously false estimations of the United States to emerge. In the commentary to his ground-breaking collection of materials on the image of America in Germany, Ernst Fraenkel referred to the severe consequences of the prejudice-ridden misjudgment of the United States. This traditional line of political thought in Germany has caused "nonsensical policies toward America to be demanded at critical historical moments by influential segments of public opinion and virtually forced through at fateful points in German history."[59] Historian Gerhard Weinberg sees the ill-advised decision to wage an unlimited submarine war prior to America's entry into the war as a sign of a virtually boundless German belief in its own superiority. Americans were regarded not only as lacking culture, but as unfit for military service. The words of Admiral Capelle express the extent of the contempt: America "is a military nullity once, twice, and three times over." That kind of blindness was no exception; it was shared by many members of the political and military class. Once it appeared, this prejudice was not to be shaken, not even by the outcome of the war. Quite the contrary, it became more and more popular. After 1945, following Germany's second defeat, it became a widespread conviction in the general population.[60] Not even Hitler took America seriously, and he would not let himself be robbed of the opportunity to declare war on the United States completely on his own. He did not believe the "ethnic jumble" [Völkergemisch] in America was capable of anything; it was not least his deep faith in the Dolchstoßlegende* that allowed him to forget, as it were, the decisive consequences of the U.S. entry into the European arena of the First World War. Even in the final months of World War II, Hitler still considered America "the land of infinite incompetence."[61]

German anti-Americanism is certainly not comprised solely of the sum of misjudgments of the United States, the results of which affected two world wars. Analyzing the deeper levels of pre-existing anti-Western attitudes provides much more insight. There, German anti-Americanism is distinguished from its counterpart in classically Western countries such as England, France, or the Nether-

---

* Dolchstoßlegende: myth of the stab in the back; the belief that Germany was betrayed by its own politicians in the First World War—trans.

lands. From a German perspective, the United States does not stand for America itself; it stands for the accumulated German traditions hostile to the idea of the West; opposition to them was not insignificant in forming the special path [Sonderweg] taken by the political culture of nineteenth-century Germany. Anti-American patterns in Germany thus reflect the depths of attitudes typical of anti-French hostilities during the anti-Napoleonic wars. Even in the early phase of East German writing, one can find traces of traditions dating back to anti-French sentiment in the so-called wars of liberation; immediately after 1945, they were nationalistically transferred to the Western occupying forces.[62]

Hostilities toward America could continue to thrive on the basis of these traditions, especially after the turn of the century, when resentment toward England was building and ideologues agitated against "Anglo-Saxon petty-mindedness." This abuse was hurled at England, but it struck America as well. The effects were increasingly apparent after the end of World War I.[63]

Anti-American hostility denounces the United States as the incarnation of a civilization whose ideas and lifestyles were soullessly cold, materialistic, technologized, and devoid of meaning to the early German identity. This characterization is by no means comprehensive in describing all phases of the German-American relationship. Relations between the two countries, and their interrelated political attitudes, are far more contradictory than can be developed while thematically concentrating on the hostilities. Actually, very different examples can also be identified—examples of an obvious affinity between Germany and the United States. In particular, the type of industrialization and modernization in the nineteenth century would soon make the country very like America in the area of material progress. Of all countries of Europe, Germany is seen as virtually the most American. And there have been long periods in which quite positive attitudes toward the United States could be observed in Germany. The Weimar Republic was very Americanized industrially and culturally, and many of its political and intellectual leaders supported this with deep conviction. It is by no means a contradiction that it is precisely those years that may be viewed as the true breeding ground of an anti-Americanism that was ideologically strengthened in Germany—on the contrary.

"No Nightingales"

ROMANTIC DISTORTIONS
IN THE NINETEENTH CENTURY

Illustration in the Karl May novel
Mutterliebe, 1899

The unholy three kings
Simplicissimus, 1916

The Age of Romanticism had a definitive influence on the German image of America. It is easy to see why the Romantics did not have very much nice to say about North America, since they considered natural rather than revolutionary development to be real and historically significant. They viewed the principles of both 1776 and 1789 as contemptible rationalism and materialism—mechanical rule of abstract institutions. By countering pure civilization with highly valued culture, they created a "gap between a European and a Western, American world that has not been bridged to this day."[64]

Although Romanticism was by no means the only relevant trend that defined elements of nineteenth-century Germany's image of America—for a period of time the pro-American position of political liberalism was predominant—Romanticism can with all justification be considered the main workshop for lasting anti-American images and metaphors. The Romantics' clear disapproval of America went hand in hand with general opposition to liberal views, with sentiments against a supposed predominance of money and materialism, and with a rejection of both "abstract" constitutional thought and freedom, which was denounced as being just as abstract. This aversion to the approaching modern age and its bastion "America" grew out of the illusion of a past—in this case, an imagined Middle Ages.

Whereas supporters of the revolutionary movement saw the Constitution of the United States as the realization of their goal with respect to their constitutional ideas, Ro-

mantics indulged in floods of invectives against America's
ideas of life and order. Hildegard Meyer's study of "North
America as judged by German writing up to the mid-nine-
teenth century" is still worthwhile reading. In it, she ana-
lyzed in detail how the Romantics provided ammunition
for criticism of America. Johann Georg Hülsemann's work
on the history of democracy in the United States, which
dealt with anti-European trends, was included in the analysis as a typical example of anti-American sentiment in Romantic circles. In his work, written in 1823—the year of the
Monroe Doctrine—Hülsemann took up the position of the
"Holy Alliance," and saw the predominant trend in North
America toward convictions of a political nature as aggressively opposed to "our religion," the monarchic, aristocratic values and attitudes of Europe. Indeed, he seemed to
find everything "'based on this transatlantic foundation'
nothing but pernicious."[65] According to Prince von Metter-
nich, the doctrine of separation of spheres of influence as
well as political values served as a way for the United
States of America to "clearly announce its intention, not
only to set power versus power, but, to put it even more
clearly, altar versus altar. This unfortunate declaration has
cast criticism and contempt at European institutions worthy of the greatest respect. . . ."[66] Hülsemann also interpreted this contrast as one of values. He felt it was not important to challenge the United States politically, but rather to
debate the American ideals of democracy and liberalism.
Hülsemann felt it was necessary to keep these away from
Europe. As long as America "stays on the far side of the
ocean, we shall wish only to view it as foreign. We shall
have to fight against it should it intervene in Europe,
should it step out aggressively and disruptively against
our primary and precious interests." The American enemy
had obviously long since penetrated the European walls of
the "Holy Alliance." Liberals started to stir—"pioneers of

the transatlantic battle formation." According to Hülsemann they were to be viewed and treated as enemies of the
state. And in fact, that "which is commonly referred to as
the battle between America and Europe" could be understood only as a battle of world views.

Such an understanding was undeniably rooted in an in-
stinctual certainty. The Romantics, assuming an idea of
community that developed naturally over time, saw the
"universal constitution of the revolutionary age" as unnatural and an "abstract freedom" in that it was oriented in
North America solely toward that which is "useful" and
"factory-made."[67] Romantic thought characterized the New
World as a haven for avarice, as the Babel of absolutely lim-
itless utilitarianism and a reprehensible absence of culture.
This type of view was represented in the made-up experiences of poet Nikolaus Lenau, who supposedly was a failure in America because of America's materialistic values.
Although having spent only a few months in the United
States in 1831/32, Lenau, feigning that he had cancelled his
plans to emigrate, provided material for legends that cut a
deep chasm in collective consciousness. Lenau's stylization
of himself as the innocent victim of the American way of
life supported the creation of effective stereotypes, especially the cultureless American. Lenau's anti-American attitude was by no means the rule in the 1830s; nevertheless
it became virtually accepted. He was immortalized in the
character of Dr. Moorfeld in Friedrich Kürnberger's 1855
Ameriphobic novel *Der Amerika-Müde* (A Man Weary of
America). Both critical and supportive traces of Lenau's anti-American railing can still be found today, over a hundred
years later. Alfred Kerr, for example, in his 1925 anthem for
America, *Yankee Land*, felt moved to refute images in the
German consciousness—traceable to Lenau—of America's
supposed lack of culture.[68] In contrast, in the novel *Niembsch oder der Stillstand* (Niembsch or the Standstill), the nov-

elist Peter Härtling extended the scope of Lenau's fictions
and his anti-American sentiment to the present day.[69] In
any case, the impact of Lenau's inventions as an apparently well-founded documentation of America's lack of culture was profound.[70] Myths spread by Lenau of contemptible materialism and cultural superficiality in America reveal a great deal about the European consciousness.

First of all, there was the official story of Lenau's suffering, with descriptions of the hair-raising state of affairs
in the New World. Most of these were depicted in the poet's published letters to his brother-in-law. Very much in
keeping with the emotional world of early Romanticism,
Lenau denounced the omnipotent commercial spirit in
America. "Brother," he wrote on October 16, 1832 to his
brother-in-law, "the petty-mindedness of these Americans
stinks to heaven. They are dead to the life of the mind,
dead as doornails."[71] In another letter he lamented the low
level of education of Americans, who show interest only in
"mercantile" and "technical" abilities. "Here, the practical
human being is developed in all its terrible rationality."[72]
Even achievements in this area in America do not represent
an "organic culture that has grown from within," but an
external, violently and rapidly developed "rootless" one. It
has nothing of its own; everything is merely put on.[73] And
he really did see everything there as rootless: farming, industry, trade, and above all the political institutions. Just as
a North American can hardly speak of a "fatherland,"
Americans can't really talk about love for the fatherland.
According to Lenau, if Americans act in the sense of their
republican constitution, this is only with the intention of
securing their private property. "That which we call fatherland is in America nothing more than security for one's
assets. The American knows nothing, seeks nothing but
money; he has no ideas; consequently, the state is not an intellectual and moral institution (fatherland), but merely a

material convention."[74] Lenau was also familiar with the idea of American degeneration. He spoke of the "true land of decline,"[75] and passed down the horror stories that had already been around for generations, that human beings and animals over there "degenerate further from generation to generation."[76]

All of this was neither new for his time nor particularly original. Such chiding of American utilitarianism and its similar British counterpart was common on the continent. Their proverbial business acumen, legal contractualism, and worldly pragmatism met with emotional disapproval. Lenau surpassed such aversions by far with the Romantic genius for exaggeration. Not only are the people robbed of their souls by materialism and business in America; nature is also a victim of alienation. And thus Americans know "no wine, no nightingales!"[77] Even the people lose all desire and ability to sing. "The nightingale is smart not to spend any time with these creatures. It seems to be profoundly significant that there are no nightingales in America; it is like a poetic curse."[78]

But the poet did not exhaust himself in criticism. Lenau, "weary of America," was driven by his apparently lamentable experiences in America to catharsis, so to speak, followed by an awakening. He said he needed the New World as a concrete contrast to the lost self, in order to find himself in the face of experienced alienation. In America, where the split "other" is at home, Lenau could rediscover his spiritual wholeness. In any case, he told his brother-in-law that his stay in America had the significance of a baptism. It led to his spiritual rebirth and an inner return to those aspects of Germany and Europe that had not received proper appreciation, and whose narrowness he had originally fled. "My stay in the New World has cured me of the chimera of freedom and independence that I had longed for with youthful enthusiasm. There I became convinced that true freedom exists only in our own hearts, in our desires and thoughts, our feelings and our actions."[79] This "German freedom," as it was later referred to, would one day represent the opposite of the principle of the "West," which stood for alienation, power, numbers, and money. And America was soon to become synonomous with the "West."

The actual "payoff" of Lenau's journey to the New World, however, was something else. The poet was certainly no poor, disappointed, and remorseful emigrant who returned to his homeland. The whole story of his suffering in America was concocted—a mere legend, admittedly a good one. The romantic adventure was nothing but a pack of lies from start to finish. Lenau never intended to emigrate to America. His trip was simply for investment purposes, that is, a business trip. His return was planned. The poet had speculated successfully with state securities and had made a considerable profit. Now he wanted to invest his unexpected wealth at favorable terms, and America was a good place to do that. Lenau intended nothing else but to buy a farm in the fertile Ohio Valley and lease it to a German emigrant; everything had already been arranged. That was considered the safest way to invest money and be assured of profits enabling a leisurely life of luxury in the Old World.

In his heart-rending letters from the New World, that which Lenau criticized "about Americans was actually his reason for going there himself. He projected his own motives for travelling to America onto American reality."[80]

Wasn't Nikolaus Lenau, a man "weary of America," really a cold, calculating speculator who on top of everything was intent on creating a far-reaching legend that would hide his own greed, and even turn it around entirely? Indeed, the trip to the land of freedom, which he denounced, was strictly for "mammon, filthy lucre." Not a trace of a ro-

mantic longing for America that could lead to disappointment. But there was an air of weltschmerz, belated love for
the homeland, and a remorseful return. The poet speculated on two things: On the one hand, his money, and on the
other, the approval of his community. Lenau knew very
well the kind of heart-rending language he would need to
arouse sympathy. It was a rather classic reaction: the tor-
mented soul is relieved of strain by burdening the "other"
with the tortured guilty conscience that comes with realizing desire. With respect to the self-alienation that developed with the emergence of modernity, America was made
a screen on which to project repressed wishes and fears.

It was appropriate for that time to grumble about supposedly typical qualities of Americans, especially avarice.
And in that, Nikolaus Lenau, the late Romantic, was not
alone; more likely he even represented a widespread way
of thinking. Hoffmann von Fallersleben's poem "Die neue
Welt" (The New World), published in 1843, speaks of the
"fetish of freedom" in America; of the "petty-minded people at the tea table"; of "swindler spirit" and "self-interest."
Matching Lenau's mood, Fallersleben wrote the following
rhyme: "And so no grapes hang from your vine / Nor do
your flowers have a scent, / No bird can even sing a line, /
And poetry its life is spent." Another author of the "Young
Germany" literary movement, Karl Gutzkow, characterized North Americans as "salesmen for one big banking
house." Heinrich Laube, a friend of Romantic poet Heinrich Heine, expressed a much more extreme image of
America in his novel *Das junge Europa* (The Young Europe).
It is a petty "business school that claims to be a world. . . .
No history, no free science, no free art! Free trade is the total freedom; . . . anything that does not bring in money is
useless, and that which is useless is unnecessary!"[81]

There was also resistance to such positions, however.
As early as 1827, Goethe dealt polemically with prevailing

anti-American tastes. In a posthumously published poem "To the United States," he honored America and rejected the criticism of the Romantics. The "living time" of the New World will counter the historicism of "dilapidated castles" and "purposeless recollection." "America, you have it better"—as its leading line.[82]

Anti-American reasoning is by no means a domain of backward-looking cultural criticism. With regard to "America," both the "Left" and the "Right" often used the same code and the same or similar images. Nevertheless, a critique of America inspired by the Enlightenment was generally more complex and more ambivalent than its conservative counterpart.

Heinrich Heine's position can be used to exemplify such closeness and distance. His brash remarks, his crudeness and sarcasm about America are well-known. In the later "Lamentations" in *Romancero* (1851), under the heading "Now, Where To?" he wrote, "I have sometimes thought to sail / To America the Free / To that Freedom Stable where / All the boors live equally. / But I fear a land where men / Chew tobacco in platoons, / There's no king among the pins, / And they spit without spittoons."[83]

But it was not only an aged, ailing, and resigned Heine who gave free rein to his wit at the expense of American democracy. As early as the July 1, 1830 entry of his *Ludwig Börne: A Memorial,* a younger Heine described America disparagingly as "that monstrous prison of freedom, where the invisible chains would oppress me even more heavily than the visible ones at home, and where the most repulsive of all tyrants, the populace, hold vulgar sway!"[84] He wrote that he used to love the country, although he had never seen it. Even now he felt he "must publicly laud it, merely out of professional duty."[85] Heine's profound age-related pessimism toward the ideals of equality, liberalism, republic, and communism can be seen in the harsh recommendation of America that he dedicated to the "dear German peasants! There are no princes or nobles there; all men are equal—equal dolts. . . ."[86] Heine felt the coexistence of slavery and the fear of God was monstrously hypocritical, a terrible legacy (later, this became a widespread topos). "They have learned this hypocrisy from the English, who incidentally have bequeathed them their worst characteristics. Worldly pursuits are their true religion, and money is their God, their only Almighty God."[87]

The image of money as an idol of alienation was a very popular motif of left-wing criticism. It could just as well have come from Moses Hess, nicknamed the Socialist Rabbi. Hess's tracing it back to national character, as Heine traced it to the British, is without a doubt a xenophobic contraction. It appears paraphrased in Marx, in the highly ambivalent work, "On the Jewish Question."[88] It is astounding how close these authors, of all people, come to expressing resentments in their use of the money metaphor in describing Jews. As far as the source of Marx's reference to money as as object of idolatry is concerned, it can most likely be assumed that Marx took this as well as other flashes of inspiration and fitting remarks from Heine, twenty years his senior and a close friend from Paris. Was Heine a source of anti-American images and crude national psychology? Such texts can only be understood properly within the context of their time. The true meaning, on the other hand, lies in the significance of America as a metaphor.

Heine also used America as a metaphor for the Other, especially for the future. America became the target of criticism that was actually meant for political opponents. And because the true addressees could not be mentioned directly for a variety of reasons, America was used as a code.

How should we understand Heine's attitude toward America, its values and lifestyles? In view of the 1830 July Revolution, he was enthusiastic about Maria Joseph

Lafayette, who became active again after witnessing two world-changing events, the American and French Revolutions. Heine elevated him to a type of Moses, who received the "ten commandments of the new world religion" in America.[89] In *Französische Zustände* (Conditions in France), published in 1832, Heine characterized Lafayette as someone capable of combining the refined manners of a French marquis and the openness of a common citizen.[90] He could bring together the best qualities of the new bourgeoisie, namely, love of equality, modesty, and honesty.[91]

This paean outburst was no accident. In 1822 Heine had professed his faith in what he called the "North American Catechism"[92]—the inviolable human rights. A short time later the United States seemed to him a likely refuge of choice for oppressed European liberals.[93] His increasing distance to America, which became perceivable in the 1930s, was—as often the case—not so much due to developments in the United States itself as to a shift in the convictions that America stood for. First of all, Heine was disappointed by the promises of liberalism in view of the class egotism that emerged within the French bourgeoisie after the July Revolution. For Heine, a republican state of, by, and for the people, which America stood for in its political symbolism, was simply no longer worthy of emulation. Further, his sarcastic remarks about America concealed yet another motif, namely, his feud with Ludwig Börne and his Parisian following. Heine had had a falling out with Börne and other German emigrants who had remained loyal to Jacobinic and even Babouvist ideals of equality. This conflict manifested itself among other things in differing attitudes toward America, the land of absolute equality or of forced conformism.[94] Heine's views were similar to the Saint-Simonists, and in his "Conditions in France" he declared himself a "royalist by inclination" who abhorred the "monotonous, colorless, and petit bourgeois way of life in America."[95] His ridicule of America was meant primarily for Börne and his philosophy of equality, which Heine mocked as a crude levelling out of society, a position which incidentally was not all that foreign to Marx either.[96]

All in all, Heine also used America as a metaphor for the future, and more and more he perceived the blessings it once promised as a curse. Contemporaries also saw "America" in this way, as meaning democracy for the masses. It cannot be denied that both the poet and "Young Germany" played a substantial role in creating the arsenal of anti-American stereotypes.[97]

Ferdinand Kürnberger had very different motives in writing the aforementioned novel, *Der Amerika-Müde*, which was based on the Lenau myth. The title alone betrays the author's intention; it was meant as an antithesis of the popular pro-American 1838 novel by Ernst Willkomm, *Die Europamüden* (Weary of Europe).[98] Kürnberger's novel is something like a literary indictment of the American state of affairs. Everywhere nothing but domination by swindlers and the worship of mammon; the stock exchange as the temple of alienation. Of course, none of this was new. But Kürnberger's work represented a qualitative intensification in that the contrast was defined in ethnic terms. The social mask had been mutated into nature. Germanness and Americanness were made into irreconcilable and unchangeable opposites.

Theoretically, there is another possible way of reading the novel, as represented by certain emancipatory currents in German studies. They understood the work as a dedicated and consistent critique of capitalism.[99] This interpretation is of course based less on the text itself than on the political position of the author. Kürnberger, son of a plebeian, had fought for the revolution in 1848/49 in Vienna and Dresden, and was released from prison in Dresden in the course of the Reich constitutional campaign in 1850. His attitude toward America thus must be appraised against this revolutionary background. Following this interpretation, his novel was directed against the Jacobinic, patriotic, republican enthusiasm for America, as was widespread among the 1848ers.

The 1848 liberals and democrats were totally supportive of the United States, and this was not only due to the fact that the USA was the only significant power that recognized the Frankfurt Parliament as a representative body and exchanged delegates with it. There were indeed profound, principled motives for showing sympathies with America, yet the revolutionaries went their separate ways after the revolution failed. Some became reactionary fanatics, and others retained their convictions.[100] In any case, participation in the 1848-49 revolution did not signify a permanent commitment to liberalism. The path taken by Richard Wagner is exemplary here, as is Kürnberger's development. The novel, published in 1855, thus needs to be read as the author wrote it, as a hyper-German and racist anti-American polemic.

In any case, it is not easy to find any social criticism in Kürnberger's epic. On the contrary, frequent contrasts referring to place of origin are obvious, such as German profundity pitted against "routine superficiality"; German warm-heartedness versus "cool American courteousness"; "German religion" countering "dry sectarianism"; German linguistic richness versus the cacophonous lack of ideas; German individuality and follow-the-herd party politics in America; German wine and American hypocrisy of restraint. The American is the "God of things"; the German is the incarnation of the spiritual. The German as the paragon of intellectual drive, "a living cathedral, an eternal hymn of enthusiasm," stands apart from the Yankee who sees the stock exchange as the "highest and most holy citadel."[101]

The interpretation of Kürnberger's "America" merely as an indictment of capitalist reality seems improbable against this background. In terms of the subsequent impact, we are more likely seeing something like a popular foundation of anti-Americanism that serves both the left and right wings to the same extent. The former sees itself as socially critical and the latter traces its enmity directly back to ethnic criteria. The fact that the two standpoints can hardly be distinguished from one another in individual cases is characteristic of the phenomenon of anti-Americanism.

Ferdinand Kürnberger was like most European critics of America in that he had of course never been to the New World. He nevertheless found a popular way of expressing the disappointment experienced by returnees who had emigrated after 1848 filled with great hopes. Kürnberger's novel was the most prominent description of German disillusionment with America, though an extensive collection of outright disappointment literature existed, such as the early work by Friedrich Otto, *Diesseits und jenseits des Oceans* (This Side and the Other Side of the Ocean, 1852). In a meanwhile familiar manner, Americans were characterized as monsters of a reprehensible and depraved lifestyle, as "dirty, petty-minded people," as "money-making animals," who wallow in the "latrine of Europe" where "greedy, petty-minded people and criminals on the lam" cavort. Panic-stricken, the author conjured up the danger of such a state of affairs spreading to Germany, as money and wheelings and dealings "have unfortunately acquired too much importance here as well."[102] Fear was lurking— fear of degeneration and decadence threatening to spread from America to Europe.

While horrors of degeneration and decadence in the eighteenth century had always been linked to natural phenomena, later visions of doom had spread to a social context. Fear of being infected by vile materialism and thus doomed to fall became widespread; it was a fear of the "negative energy of the American national spirit" that could extend beyond its own borders. "America represents a dreadful danger to all of humanity. This danger must be recognized if its spirit is not to gain the upper hand, driving all development to ruin."[103]

Fear of the decline of the natural world and anti-civilization phobias came together in so-called "Indian literature," which was avidly read in Europe and above all in Germany. Native American Indians, "who lived rugged, trusting, and unspoiled lives according to the ways of their tribes, yet fought a losing battle against colonists and technicians, [were] not only the stuff of fables and idyll for the writers, but the vision of an ideal life as well."[104] The original America embodied nature, and Europe invading America was the unnatural. The Native American was the unspoiled, naturally noble and courageous individual "in contrast to the false and greedy white man."[105] Such an attitude is not particularly surprising, as those showing sympathies for the "noble savage" actually identified themselves with him.[106] For the public, it rarely had anything to do with real Native Americans, who served popular imaginations first and foremost as an identifying counter-metaphor to ruthlessly advancing modernity. Enthusiasm for the epic way of life of native North Americans did not really take off until the first third of the nineteenth century through the works of James Fenimore Cooper, which were devoured by readers.[107] They were gripped by the heroic tragedy of Cooper's characters, who tried in vain to escape the merciless assault of a materialistic civilization. This identification with Native American culture articulated the readers' own fears of surging modernity. The "good white man," characterized by the aging Leatherstocking, leaves the colony of his countrypeople to go westward in search of the lost way of life. He cannot tolerate the devastated forests, the starving animals, and the unjust treatment of Native Americans by the civilized New England residents.

Cooper's popularity was by no means limited to the Old World. His works were also honored as epics of colonization by his compatriots. The underlying tone of sadness in Cooper's works might have served as a compensatory relief from the burden of moral ambivalence in American frontier culture.

Similar and yet with a very different focus were the imaginative "Indian" stories by Karl May. May set out to provide social criticism in the form of a direct contrast between noble nature and degenerate society. His idealized "Indian" stories depicted a "White Man" striving in all directions for money. His utilitarian and self-centered thoughts and actions, undermining the natural tribal order, knew no bounds. But May did not consider all whites reprehensible. He distinguished between active farmers, and especially nature-loving wilderness heroes, on the one hand, and profit-hungry Yankees, on the other. The Yankee represented avarice and slyness, as it were, capitalism *per se*.[108] Old Surehand, May's contrasting identification figure, crusaded against "Western civilization."[109] Karl May took this to an extreme. Whenever he described Americans, with the exception of the nature-loving western frontier men, the subject was profit. May regarded the Yankee as the epitome of capitalism.

However, the Native American is not always a symbol of that which is good and natural in literature critical of America. Starting at the end of the nineteenth century, after obviously having lost their naturalness, Native Americans, or rather, the qualities of the syncretistic American that have been attributed to Native Americans, also stood for disastrous compulsiveness, degeneration, and decline.

Friedrich Nietzsche, who was otherwise rather unim-
pressed by the spirit of the times, linked untamed nature
and anti-natural civilization in his image of the degenerate
Native American. In *The Gay Science* (1881/82), he wrote
disparagingly, "Leisure and idleness—There is somethings
of the American Indians, something of the ferocity peculiar
to the Indian blood, in the American lust for gold; and the
breathless haste with which they work—the distinctive
vice of the new world—is already beginning to infect old
Europe with its ferocity and is spreading a lack of spiritu-
ality like a blanket. . . ."[110]

Anti-American clichés developed in the period from
1815 up to the Revolution of 1848/49 and they have persisted to varying degrees to the present day.[111] While the
last third of the eighteenth century can be regarded as the
incubation period, specifically prejudicial metaphors
emerged during the first half of the nineteenth century to
protect against bourgeois lifestyles and capitalist economic
forms. Anti-Americanism in politics developed analogous
to this. As long as political liberalism continued to have a
lasting impact on economically upwardly mobile classes,
America and the values associated with it received respect
and recognition. This of course applied to an enlightened
critic of capitalism like Karl Marx, who saw achieving capitalism as a precondition for overcoming it and saw the
United States itself as "the youngest and yet most powerful representative of the West."[112] In the tradition of the
1848ers, he finally invited the United States to intervene in
reactionary Europe. To Marx, it did not seem a long way off
to a future socialist society from the people's rule that was
manifested by the republican democracy in the United
States.

It was predominantly the left-wing liberals who continued to view the United States as the most progressive
country in the world and as a haven for free trade and

bourgeois civilization.[113] They praised American principles and the ideal of the American system of government—the system that was "abstract," "dead," and "rigid," and thus a horror for the Romantics, the very repugnant "abstract freedom" of an alienating world. Supporters of such freedom, on the other hand, could refer to Alexander von Humboldt, who very early on informed the Prussian king of the advantages of representative government, using the United States as an example. "Your Majesty, it is a form of rule that no one sees or feels and yet it is much more powerful than Your Majesty's rule."[114] Carl Schurz expressed it in a similar way in a letter. In America, he claimed, you could see every day, "how little is necessary in ruling a people. Indeed, the anarchy which one shudders to mention in Europe exists here in full bloom. Truly there are governments, but no masters. . . ."[115]

Later on, attitudes supportive of America also became popular. At any rate, it was Social Democratic Party leader Wilhelm Liebknecht in 1887 who, with fatherly forbearance, rebuked those Social Democrats who attacked the constitution of the United States. In an article for the Party newspaper that was critical yet sympathetic, he wrote, "'You overestimate these Americans,' a compatriot who has been living in the New World for quite some time told me recently, 'Americans are terribly narrow-minded people, arch-conservatives.' The well-meaning compatriot had gotten carried away with words and prejudice, as I tried in vain to make clear to him. Americans truly are 'arch-conservative' in a political sense, but that is not because of narrow-mindedness; rather, there is a very good reason for it. All democratic peoples are conservative. The American constitution has truly earned the right to be 'conserved'— in spite of everything. Despotically ruled peoples are never conservative, because they are not content. Only democratic peoples can be conservative, a darned simple truth

that so many so-called statesmen simply cannot understand."[116]

Around the turn of the century there was a noteable increase in anti-American sentiment. Whereas Social Democratic theorist Karl Kautsky made a passionate, republican
testimonial to the United States as late as 1906, calling it
"the freest country in the capitalist sphere"[117] and thus in
the world, a growing uneasiness was noticeable within
business circles. References to the "American threat" became legion. This shift in attitude in 1900 might have been
tied to the first major loan that Germany took out in the
United States. The idea of taking out a loan was indeed
new. Up to that time it had been the other way around;
North America had been the preferred investment region
for the export of German capital. Now the relationship was
apparently reversing itself and the United States was
viewed as a threatening economic competitor. This shift
was not only perceived in Germany. Complaints could also be heard in England about the American threat—despite new political relations between the two powers that
had been celebrated at the turn of the century as the "Great
Rapproachment." In any case, all of a sudden word spread
of "Americanization" and thus the conspiracy of an American threat to European culture and lifestyles.

In 1901 British journalist William Thomas Stead published a well-heeded study, "The Americanization of the
World or the Trend of the Twentieth Century." Stead saw
the term he coined as a metaphor for the industrial and
commercial modern age; he thus created a term that
has been used since the fin de siècle. "Americanization"
evoked nightmares of an emerging mass society—the rule
of misanthropic rationalization and a trivial mass culture
that destroys all individuality.[118]

Such visions of horror were received with open arms,
especially in Germany. Wilhelm von Polenz's 1903 travel

log with the revealing title, *Das Land der Zukunft* (The Land of the Future), warned Germans of emulating America in any way. "For the Old World and especially for Germany that would mean sinking from a higher level of culture to a lower one. Americanization of culture means trivialization, mechanization, stupification."[119] The author saw America as reflecting nothing but its anticipated image.

The fact that the United States continued to lose esteem had to do with the "world politics" of Wilhelm II. In particular the Spanish-American War, the Samoan and Venezuelan conflicts, and Mexico's war with the United States all served to worsen regard for the United States in German public opinion. Pan-Germanism was primarily responsible for the trend. The moderate conservatives, liberals, and social democrats wanted to make a settlement with the United States, but the political strategy of strengthening German-American relations while bypassing England proved a failure. And so the two Anglo-Saxon powers gradually became part of the public consciousness, which emphasized their similarity. Pronounced anti-Americanism came to the surface in full force with the tremendous break brought on by the First World War.[120]

By no means did full-blown hostility grow solely out of war-related political or military opposition. Rather, a slow yet steady consciousness raising can be traced, that finally, impetuously opened the floodgates in 1917. Enough bad feelings had accumulated leading up to the catastrophic event, having been nurtured by the underlying images and myths of the first half of the nineteenth century. The alienation of modernity was projected onto everything foreign, in Germany more than elsewhere. While in the classical Western countries, development of lifestyle and consciousness managed to keep up with changes in the material world, there was a considerable lag in Germany. Tremendous progress in the areas of economics, science, and technology was offset by ways of thinking oriented toward the past as a means of compensation. Intense ideological feelings mushroomed that were opposed to civilization and enlightenment, rationalism and materialism, technology and progress, industrialization and urbanization. Growth of economic and political power was combined with a pledge to an ideal world of rootedness and loyalty to the homeland, of service and duty, of tradition and community.

Because developments in Germany were out of sync, the linking of differences to corresponding political mentalities was contradictory. "The West" was then seen in Germany as culturally different, as foreign. America itself was not yet an important topic of discussion. On the contrary, much less malice was felt toward the United States than toward the western European powers, England and France. Modris Ekstein's definitive study on political and cultural thought before and during the First World War found that global wrestling in the consciousness of the warring nations actually represented a "civil war of the European middle class."[121] It was justified as an unavoidable decision between contradicting value systems and their corresponding ways of life. The educated classes in Germany opposed the ideas and values of the West as superficial and hypocritical. "What English and French ethics have to say about liberalness and equality is nothing but hypocritical rhetoric, nothing but lies and deception. They hide the dictatorship of form that manifests itself in the Gallic obsession with good taste and the British fixation on trade and business." This was then countered by German authenticity that recognizes reality, not with eyewash and swindle, but with truth, with essence as opposed to appearance, with totality instead of norms.[122] Hostility towards Anglo-Saxons was directed primarily at England, which provided competition for Germany and barred it from its claim to "a place in the sun." Although traditional anti-English sentiment and anti-Americanism are structurally similar, hostility toward the United States also includes cultural aversion. England was despised as the "perfidious Albion," but despite all the attributed petty-mindedness, the globally trading nation was recognized as having a sort of aristocratic culture. America, on the other hand, was seen both culturally and socially as a lower class artificially inflated to a nation. It was thus much more humiliating to be inferior to America, a colonial nation of hybrids, as this was combined with nightmares of degeneration and decline. The United States' entry into World War I, the German defeat in the fall of 1918, and the Versailles Treaty caused a relatively subliminal negative image of America to mushroom into posting America as the ideological enemy.[123]

"Wilson is Great and Kautsky is his Prophet"

WEIMAR AMBIVALENCES

Ibsen's 100th birthday;
"Once I was as famous as this guy".
Simplicissimus, 1928

Beautiful Perspectives: New York Suffragettes
decide to forgo high fashion
Simplicissimus, 1913

"The World War unbalanced us emotionally. The psychological effect of the fact that America tipped the scales
in a wrestling match that neither European camp came out
of as the strongest nation—an imponderable situation,
which occasionally increased America's influence out of all
proportion—was not to be forgotten overnight."[124] This is
how the author of the most widely-read 1920s German
book on America sketched the motivation behind the surging anti-Americanism. And that at a time when interest in
America was increasing at "epidemic" proportions.[125] In
fact, America did not become "a real problem" for Germany until during the Weimar Republic.[126] Adolf Halfeld's
book *Amerika und der Amerikanismus* (America and Americanism) was not published until 1927. The mood that it expressed was not only a reaction to the defeat; it also reflected what in the 1920s was regarded in both a negative and
a positive sense as "Americanization." For the most part
this referred to the economic infiltration of Germany by
American capital and the onslaught of mass culture associated with America. Economic independence and cultural
identity seemed to be threatened by the peace agreement
and American loan policy.

Marked hatred for Wilson was typical of anti-Americanism during the Weimar Republic. Propaganda against
his policies mobilized all the characterizations that had traditionally been held against Anglo-Saxons in Germany:
falseness, sanctimoniousness, and hypocrisy.[127] Woodrow
Wilson as a person was confronted with nothing short of
foaming rage in political writings from just about all polit-

ical parties and camps. He was almost unanimously accused of that very "typical Anglo-Saxon" treachery, which from a German perspective always spoke of iron principles and meant nothing more than Mammon, filthy lucre—or as Theodor Fontane quipped about the British, they would speak of Christ and mean calico.[128] Adolf Halfeld, who earned the dubious honor of being the most significant representative of literary anti-Americanism during the Weimar period, put it this way: "The peculiar two-sidedness in American life—idealistic pathos paired up with crafty business practices; the religious foundations of ambition; the preacher who is an entrepreneur; the proselytizer of morals; the businessman with God and ideals on his lips; the Fourteen Points; world peace with Wall Street's seal of approval—in the end it all goes back to the Puritan ethic, the ethic of the self-liberating bourgeoisie."[129] The ethic of the self-liberating bourgeoisie is traced back to the unity of faith and business—seen here as a dichotomy—that is typical of American culture, influenced by Puritanism and Calvinism. The contradiction between declared principles and pragmatic actions, however, was associated with the essence of a "petty-minded nation." According to hostile opinions, the soul of such a nation was personified by the American president, Woodrow Wilson, who was branded as the chief hypocrite and fake.

Aside from hatred for Wilson and a national psychology that was strongly influenced by trends, another motive for anti-Americanism appeared during the 1920s: America was accused of "imperialism." This referred primarily to American loan policy that came in the wake of the Dawes Plan (1924) and provided the basis for the economic prosperity of the "Golden Twenties." The Dawes Plan was denounced by "anti-imperialist" agitators as a conspiracy to "enslave" Germany. They used images and slogans that were later taken up by National Socialist publications as well as the radical Left.

Profound disappointment in the United States was essentially the result of self-deception. In particular, the German Military High Command did everything in its power to hide the whole truth about the war. Actually, the drama started over the unlimited use of German submarines against the commercial fleets of other countries, which unquestionably provoked America's entry into the war.

It was well-known in Germany that an unlimited submarine war would pull the United States into the world war, but anyone who dared to refer to the military consequences of intervention by the powerful American forces and the increased threat that would result for Germany was dismissed as a killjoy. Especially with respect to American military capability, all warnings were arrogantly thrown to the winds. But as soon as the first fresh U.S. troops appeared in the European theater, everyone screamed betrayal and insinuated that they were motivated by purely material interests. It was said that the United States only entered the war to assure American plutocrats that the war loans they made to the Allies would be repaid, despite the threat of a German victory. *Gebhard*, the standard handbook of German history, recorded in 1923 that the deciding factor for the United States to enter the war was the "close ties of American high finance and industry to the Entente."[130] This economic interpretation was given a polemic thrust from the moment people wrongly started feeling deceived by Wilson and believing in a victory on the battlefield. But the American president had more likely saved Germany from a total military defeat. In the end it was the Military High Command that pushed the Reich government in the fall of 1918 to approve Wilson's Fourteen Points from January of that year and to enter into cease-fire negotiations. The military chief of staff, fully aware of the German army's constitution, knew that a devastating defeat would have otherwise been inevitable. This fact was always wisely kept secret from the public. Based on a patently false assumption, the German public thus believed that the cease-fire was only accepted on the condition that Wilson agree to guarantee Germany a just peace— i.e., one reaffirming the status quo. Otherwise there was supposedly an option to continue armed battle. Across the entire political spectrum, it was an almost unanimously believed that the German people laid down their arms because they trusted in Wilson's promise, and despite all their trust they were betrayed by the shameful Treaty of Versailles. The American president thus became a secular Judah figure for his German critics.

In his study of German-American relations during the Weimar Republic, Peter Berg followed up the pioneeering work by Ernst Fraenkel, examining the similarities and differences in the central themes of anti-Americanism in Germany. Both the metaphor of betrayal and the image of a world-dominating plutocracy are part of a paranoid ideology with "America" at its center and Woodrow Wilson as its treacherous agent. "Finance capital," pulling the strings behind the scenes of international politics, belonged to the jargon of both the right and the left wings.

Many people discovered American "hypocrisy" right after the United States entered the war. Adolf von Harnack, for example, said the following in May 1917: "As soon as our enemies had shortages in ammunition and everything that goes into fighting a war, yes even earlier, democratic pacifism supplied everything in surplus. The bullets that passed through our heroes were probably more often American than British, French, or Russian ones. At the same time, Wilson called for a day of prayer for peace."[131] Eduard Meyer, scholar of ancient history, who had already welcomed the unlimited submarine war with "enthusiasm,"[132] wrote the following after the peace treaty was signed in August 1919: "To Germany, Wilson remains a type of unctuous hypocrite who brings together everything that contradicts the German nature and is loathsome to the core. But he will be remembered in the history of the world as the man who, by assuming a doctrinaire arrogance enabling him to redirect world history through imperious intervention, not only destroyed the ideals that Germany sought to achieve, but became the executioner of European culture in his submission to France's wild vindictiveness and England's cold-hearted egotism. He has contributed more than any other mortal to the age of steadily growing barbarism descending on the white race, in which the culture that Europe created has been irretrievably doomed."[133]

Disappointment in Wilson from the center of the political spectrum was expressed in, for example, the *Deutsche Allgemeine* newspaper: "In view of the dreadful conditions laid out in the peace treaty, it must be said that no rape and no degradation suffered at the hands of our enemies could disappoint the German people as utterly as the knowledge that Wilson apparently deceived us."[134] Even *Vorwärts* (Forward), the mainstream Social Democratic Party newspaper, reported after the Paris treaty terms were disclosed that "the mask has now officially been ripped from the face" of the Entente powers, especially America, which, "in the beautiful words of Wilson, unctuously announced justice, peace under the law, lasting peace, reconciliation, etc." And now they were impudently continuing the very hypocrisy with which they had earlier wrested the weapons out of Germany's hands. International capitalism was celebrating its victory in Germany while a humiliated population foot the bill. And elsewhere the shout was heard, "They betrayed us miserably!"[135]

Those Independent Social Democrats who had declared their support for Wilson's peace proposals early on found themselves in a difficult situation. Because of their sympathies for Wilson they were severely attacked by both left and right wings. Karl Kautsky, who was favorably disposed toward the pacifist ideas of the American president and impressed by Anglo-Saxon political culture in general, was heaped with scorn in the radical left-wing *Spartacus Briefe*. The denunciatory headline read "Wilson is great, and Kautsky is his prophet."[136]

After the cease-fire was signed in November 1918, the spokespeople of what would become the Communist Party saw Wilson's peace program as nothing but a conspiracy to stabilize the imperialist countries weakened during the war. In view of the triumphant reception that the Liberal and Social Democratic Parties, in particular, gave Wilson when he arrived in Europe, Paul Levi wrote the following for the *Rote Fahne* (Red Flag): "Mr. Wilson, that miracle man who has been praised a thousandfold, coolly accepts all the homage paid to him, only then to do exactly what is demanded by the interests of the capitalists in his country and its allies."[137] Years later, during the preliminary negotiations for the Dawes Plan, the right-wing newspaper, *Deutsche Zeitung*, argued along a similar vein. Wilson was characterized "as an obedient tool of the financial powers that viewed the Great War as a major financial operation," and as a "puppet of big banking and the interests of millionaires, who had the task of creating the idealistic fig leaf for shameless profiteering."[138] Friedrich Naumann, a National Liberal, expressed support during the war for ambitious military goals. He saw the peace treaty as the establishment of a "British-American world domination system" and in all seriousness he felt that capitalism had not been introduced in Germany until that time.[139] Incidentally, that attitude reappeared, surprisingly enough, after World War II. Peter Berg referred to Naumann's popular view that the German defeat cleared the way for the definitive advance of Anglo-Saxon imperialism and capitalist exploitation. This interpretation quickly became a common motif in contemporary journalism.

Even after the United States retreated after 1920 from its position as caretaker in world politics—a move that was disastrous for Europe—Wilsonian idealism was still condemned in Germany, though now the criticism, ranging from disparaging to hostile, was directed against the League of Nations. Evidence of this widespread trend can be found in an article titled "Amerikanischer Imperialismus und deutsche Vorkriegspolitik" (American Imperialism and German Prewar Politics, 1922), by Emil Daniels. Daniels intended to show that the ideas of the League of Nations had the sole purpose of weakening national feelings and watering down patriotic spirit into vague enthusiasm. "Truly, this plutocratic, ochlocratic America has statesmen from whom even the shrewdest monsignors of the Curia in the age of dragoons and the imperial beatifiers could have learned something."[140] According to Friedrich Naumann, in the now-established system of Anglo-Saxon and imperialistic supremacy—a downright "syndicate"—the only accomplishment of the League of Nations was balancing out rivalries among its members. World peace, to be guaranteed by the League of Nations, only served to secure "world annuity operations." War in the future would amount to a revolt against the profits of the ruling peoples and their bodyguards, according to Berg's paraphrasing of Naumann's view. This totally new world order would be an Anglo-Saxon earnings order and Germany would be relegated to the status of the homeworker among the nations. Naumann thus became the ideological spokesperson for the contrast between "young" and "old nations" (Moeller van den Bruck), that is, countries designated as haves and have-nots, which was so significant in the 1930s. This was the fertile earth into which the anti-capitalist and anti-colonial rhetoric of the Right, which was to become generalized under Nazism, took root.[141]

In their impact, the Wilson myth and the "legend of the stab in the back" were like anti-democratic "Siamese twins," as coined by Ernst Fraenkel.[142] The "stab-in-the-back legend" was directed inwardly against Marxists, pacifists, and Jews. The Wilson myth (i.e., his characterization as an Anglo-Saxon hypocrite who thus revealed the essense of Puritanism and Calvinism) was directed outwards. In both myths, those out to ruin Germany had the same qualities; they stood for the power of money, interest, the stock exchange, and circulation—the epitome of capitalism. This phenomenon of ideological consciousness now started to clearly merge anti-Americanism and anti-Semitism. In its radical form, the United States was seen to represent a bastion of Jewish world domination. That which emerged directly after World War I as a product of pan-German tradition was later to become a consistent world view for the Nazis.

It became commonplace to characterize America, according to the words of Werner Sombart, as a "state of Jews" (*Judenstaat*).[143] In particular after Taft's presidency, this view saw the "Jewish" influence on public life in the United States as having gained the upper hand. Jews were thought to pull the strings in the trade unions, which were also centers of power and influence. During the war they succeeded in moving into big capital and supposedly profitted substantially from Allied war loans. Jews were also believed to have a considerable intellectual influence. In early nationalist literature, for example, Wilson's Fourteen Points were depicted as a product of Jewish minds.[144] The "enslavement" of Germany was also ascribed to the Jews, no doubt about it. Supposedly, it was not a coincidence that Wilson appointed Bernard Baruch, a Jewish financial magnate, to his cabinet. Baruch was also chosen to be Wilson's chief advisor at the Versailles conference outside of

Paris.[145] Nazi writer Giselher Wirsing later reported that the "financial provisions of the Versailles Diktat that meant to bleed Germany" were essentially the work of Baruch.[146] A brochure published in the 1940s by the Reichsführer-SS with the programmatic title "Amerikanismus—Eine Welt-gefahr" (Americanism—a World Threat), elaborated on this view even further. Bernhard Menasse (sic!) Baruch was referred to as "Wall Street Pirate No. 1" He was "one of the notorious organizers of the blockade against Germany in World War I. As one of Roosevelt's chief advisors he once again campaigned for war, in order to earn further millions as a 'big-time speculator' and to establish Jewish world domination."[147] The image of Jews responsible for Germany's ruin brings another person to mind, namely, Henry Morgenthau, Roosevelt's secretary of finance during World War II, who was accused of striving to destroy Germany economically, out of a thirst for revenge. In the later Nazi period, Roosevelt himself was the object of invective that had been reserved for Wilson up until that time. The continuation of the images seems like repetition compulsion.

Aside from the anti-Wilson element, another theme that played an important role for anti-American agitation was "imperialism," conjured up to the same extent by both the extreme Left and Right. The pattern of debate was largely based on a polemic interpretation of the Dawes Plan, which aimed to reduce the German burden of reparations and spur an economic boom with American investment capital. Thus the German economy inevitably became greatly dependent on the United States, which was redefined by the extremist agitation as proof of national submission and subjugation.

Agitation against Dawes and American capital exported to Germany might have had different motivations for the right-wing and the extreme left-wing, but the difference blurs when the similar rhetorical images and metaphors are taken into account. This synchronization of otherwise mutually exclusive political positions can only be understood with respect to an event that preceded the Dawes Plan and triggered a peculiar national harmony in Germany: the French and Belgian occupation of the Ruhr basin in 1923.

Under the direction of then French Prime Minister Raymond Poincaré, France attempted to collect outstanding German reparations payments in the form of natural resources such as coal and timber. Resistance to the French action by the German public was based on a united front against "Entente imperialism," which temporarily brought together the German Communist Party and the National Socialists. The atmosphere was reminiscent of August 1914. The rhetoric born during the "Ruhr battle" and the corresponding images and metaphors in political discourse persisted in the campaign against the Dawes Plan. Germany was portrayed as the victim of an imperialist monster, based on the model of oppression of Central American banana republics. Whereas the right wing sounded somewhat quaint when speaking of "Anglo-Saxon" world domination, the Left modernized the subject with the concept of imperialism. But in the end it was one and the same. This was apparent in popular coinages such as "Anglo-Saxon world imperialism" or the variant that emphasized the plutocratic aspect, "dollar imperialism."

A sophistocated theoretical combination of right- and left-wing world views is exemplified in Arthur Salz's *Der Imperialismus der Vereinigten Staaten* (The Imperialism of the United States). It appeared in 1923 in the renowned *Archiv für Sozialwissenschaft und Sozialpolitik* (Archives for the Social Sciences and Social Policy) and was widely received. *Dollar Diplomacy,* by two left-wing American authors, Scott Nearing and Joseph Freeman, was translated into German in 1927 and considered the catechism of contemporary anti-imperialism. The book offered a critical assessment of the involvement of U.S. capital and government in Latin America, which certainly did not set a moral example. The difficulty of transferring a discourse that developed in an American context to a totally different German context is apparent in the preface to the German edition, written by the geopolitician Karl Haushofer.[148] The extent to which Haushofer instrumentalized this originally internal critique of America can be seen in a diary entry from 1918. Here his deep-seated animosity becomes plain: ". . . for the British, existence is what is still at stake. I'll accept the idea of hatred versus hatred. But the Americans are really the only nation on earth that I view instinctively with a deep hatred—like a false, voracious, sanctimonious, shameless beast of prey that deceives with every expression and in reality only snaps around looking for food for its insatiable, dollar-lusting belly like an alligator."[149]

A type of far-reaching identification with Central and South America as victims of the North Americans emerged in the debate over reparations and loan policy. This traditional line of identification, incidentally, has persisted well into the period of the Federal Republic. Especially the popular anti-American literature, such as the works by Leo L. Matthias mentioned earlier in this book, sound like continuations of polemics from the 1920s, whose impact stretched into the 1960s and 1970s, a time when the word "imperialism" once again rose to the status of a comprehensive interpretation. In retrospect it seems as if those authors were downright plagiarized.

While the nationalist factions in the 1920s bewailed above all a supposed loss of independence of German capital and the internationalization of investment policy, the Left indulged in opportunistic, nationalist-sounding social agitation. The Dawes Plan was denounced in a way far more befitting the Right. The organ of the Communist Par-

ty, *Rote Fahne* referred to Germany as a "vassal state" of the
Americans. Another periodical, the *Internationale*, announced that the "kings of finance capital" were preparing
to convert Europe into a "new type of colony of the United
States of America." Generally, the communists felt the
Dawes Plan was an "agreement between thieves," who un-
dertook a campaign to pillage the international proletariat.
In view of the preceding "Ruhr battle" and national unity,
the propaganda of the German Communist Party was even
more shrill. In a speech before the Reichstag on March 7,
1923, Clara Zetkin received a spontaneous ovation and se-
cured support from the Right when she said in heated,
national-Bolshevist style that England, France, and the
United States wanted "to convert Germany into a colony."
Making use of traditional anti-American images mixed
with a few thoroughly appropriate assessments, Zetkin announced before the Reichstag that "the United States represents capitalists that are so shrewd, so ruthless, so lacking in old traditions that sometimes still hold back the capitalists in Europe, that they would be the last to trip over a
thread of moral reservation. No, industry, backed with
American capital, to gain control of the German labor force
as cheap labor and thus turn Germany into a colony of the
United States. (That's true!—Right). No illusions about this
fact."[150]

The "anti-imperialist" truce between the extreme Left
and Right produced some embarassing effects. This included anti-Semitism, simply because of its structural similarities. At a political event held jointly by the German
Communist Party and the Nationalists *(Völkischen)*, Ruth
Fischer did not refrain from openly using anti-Jewish arguments to gain a tactical advantage. "You are organizing
against Jewish capital, gentlemen? Whoever opposes Jewish capital, gentlemen, is engaging in class struggle, even if
he is not aware of it. You are opposed to Jewish capital and

want to defeat the stockjobbers? Then carry on. Beat down the Jewish capitalists; hang them from the lampposts; trample them down. But gentlemen, what do you think of the big capitalists, Stinnes, Klöckner. . . ?"[151]

Anti-Semitism was seen as a transition stage to correct class consciousness. Accordingly, the nationalist right wing was not moving in the wrong direction; they merely stopped halfway. Such an interpretation is nothing new, and it depicts the social democracy around the turn of the century far more accurately than normally assumed. The reference to anti-Semitism as "socialism of the stupid guys," which was falsely attributed to August Bebel though would surely have been accepted by him, essentially meant nothing more than a regret that aversion to Jewish capitalists was not extended to the moneyed class in general.[152] Nevertheless, the Social Democrats (SPD), as the most "western" of all significant political parties in Germany, always saw themselves as opponents of anti-Semitism. This was also reflected in their attitude toward America.

The SPD viewed the Dawes Plan as a triumph of reason. Nevertheless, with western support, provisos were imposed on French policies concerning the reparations issue that helped pave the way for the Pact of Locarno. In view of the occupation of the Ruhr area, however, voices were heard within SPD ranks that gave in to anti-American nationalistic propaganda and saw Germany as the victim of imperialist pillaging. In an article in the right-leaning social democratic *Glocke* with the revealing title, "Amerikanische Vorbilder der Ruhrbesetzung" (American models for the Ruhr occupation), the question was posed whether the United States could even be trusted. Would it thwart France's and Belgium's plans in the Ruhr area purely out of idealism: "two countries that are merely—even if to a larger extent—playing the same game in Germany as the United States is in South America," namely, "negative sanctioning through brutal, imperialist policy?" The right-leaning journal, *Zeitschrift für Geopolitik*, resorted to similar analogies, for example: "We are being treated in the same way as Nicaragua, Santo Domingo, Haiti, Cuba, etc."[153] It was up to Germany to blow the whistle on "Shylock's sham." The author apparently knew what he was talking about; in any case he didn't depart from the traditional image.

The analogy between the imperialist invasion of Central America and the occupation of the Ruhr area was also maintained by the impressively successful author of the Nazi period, Giselher Wirsing. In the most popular Third Reich book about America, he declared with racist imagery that the role "played by the American marines in South America was assumed by the French nigger regiments on the Rhine and the Ruhr."[154]

The anti-imperialism that united the Right and extreme Left following the Ruhr battle and the Dawes Plan incorporated both anti-western and anti-modern prejudicial metaphors. This enemy, imperialism, did not represent the consequences of abstract economic relationships that arose essentially from a productivity gap on the world market. Instead, it was an expression for a definite power with a definite name—the United States—and a definite place—America. This concept was used to connote the rationalizing global meaning of anti-Americanism, that is, exploitive plutocracy, or power thinly veiled in money. Arthur Salz, mentioned earlier, gave this hostility the necessary scholarly foundation. He felt present-day American imperialism represented nothing more than a variant of domination by finance capital. Behind the state, which embodied the general will of the people, the interests of the big New York banks were actually the driving force. According to Salz, the government yielded coweringly to the capitalists. It left the instruments of state power in their hands—army, navy, and the administrative machinery. This form of imperialism was supposedly characterized by a peculiar elasticity, allowing its victims the "appearance of political independence." Salz felt this form of imperialism was also served by the illusion of justice. In fact, "legality" was the primary asset of modern imperialism.

Anti-American images with an anti-imperialistic touch have a long shelf life. Laden with hostility, Salz's findings could just as well been written today. He wrote that "it is self-evident that the United States does missionary work with the words 'law and order.' The freedom of helpless peoples is far too meager a commodity for it even to be considered along with pillars like law and order. But experience has shown what comes with the creation of such 'cells of order.'"[155]

The short political spring of the Weimar Republic owed a great deal to America. Thanks to the "Americanization" of its industrial production sites, Germany was considered the most modern country in Europe at the end of the 1920s—Karl Kraus coined the word "Fordschritt" as a pun on the German word for progress, "Fortschritt."[156] American models were also adopted in the cultural sphere. In art and music, and especially popular culture, Germany had become "All-American." It is not surprising that, especially in the right-wing camp, such a development was not well received and was negatively judged as part of "Americanism."[157] In this regard Adolf Halfeld, an extensively cited critic of America, became well-known as an important analyst and popular sloganeer. His book on America and Americanism was regarded a bestseller. Although it offered nothing new, its impact on the zeitgeist cannot be overestimated. His caricature of democracy in America was superb in the way it took advantage of the anti-parliamentary atmosphere of the Weimar Republic. Totally in keeping with existing prejudices, he described how U.S. politics functioned: as a matter of course, votes are bought in order "to railroad through profitable laws," officials are bribed, concessions are bought, and voters are terrorized.[158] He even used the widespread anti-American theme of "forced conformity." In his view, everything in America was subjected to "unbridled business idealism"; blind "efficiency" prevailed, which of course led to a decadent levelling of culture. "Everyone wears the same suit, boots, colors, and collars; they all read the same magazines and, without actually realizing it, they are all the same product of a desolate conformity hallowed by machines and propaganda, which knows no limits."[159] Halfeld also warned of another threat to occidental culture posed by America-dominated western civilization: the equality of women and their social advancement into positions that would best be reserved for men. Women infiltrated the male domain particularly in the area of education, he believed, but they were also in the process of moving into the administration, into the very heart of the state.

The connection that some authors drew between a levelling out "middle-class morality," the Puritan, Calvinist work ethic, the materialism of a "success culture"[160] and a supposed rule by women in America is very fascinating. They felt that materialism in America was proof of the psychological dominance of women to the extent that they encourage men to focus on earning money. On the other hand, loss of masculinity was considered directly connected to all that is pecuniary and mercantile. In the end, the "American religion of work" is what was considered responsible for the fact that women achieved dominance over men. The "inferiority of men" was referred to as the "main characteristic of the American social order."[161] Jews were depicted as the original puritans, the "inventors of work." Thus it is not surprising that "Jewish and American spirits" merged in materialism.[162] This in turn emerged from mechanization and feminization—a way of life that had succeeded in taking over America.

While Hermann Graf Keyserling used the contrast of "male society" and "female society" to lament the decline of aristocratic values and the victory of the bourgeoisie, letting it all flow together in anti-American speech, Halfeld went much further in his misogynist polemic. He, too, complained of the supposed rule by women in the United States, blaming men for having a servile, subservient attitude. American men, in Halfeld's view, seriously believed that women have a "moral, aesthetic, and intellectual advantage." This didn't surprise Halfeld, since he believed that the ideal of equality, utilitarianism, and the quest for money have downright robbed men of their natural attributes. Their "male aggression" has been "repressed by the puritanical traits of the race," and "a conventional weakness instinct" towards women has become second nature. Besides that, the author reminded readers "that in school, the most important pillar of American civilization, women have just about been crowned the absolute rulers." The threat of such a system to "the creative intelligence of men, the confirmation of their judgment, the naturalness of awakening sexuality, and the future prospects of society can be seen everywhere in the American world."[163] Even Nazi ideologue Alfred Rosenberg could only agree with such findings. He said, "The consequence of women's rule in America is the nation's conspicuously low level of culture."[164] In addition to "materialistically" grounded explanations of women's domination in the United States, anti-American misogynists introduced an additional reason why women assumed power: the matriarchal culture of Native American tribes.[165]

C.G. Jung also recognized a Native American cultural influence in the collective psyche of Americans. In everything the Americans want, he said, "the Indian aspects are visible"—especially in sports. Nothing but Indian initiations could compete with the "ruthlessness and cruelty of a rigorous American practice session." Jung saw not only an "Indian" influence but a "Negro" one as well—"a psychological influence, of course, without mixing blood." In any case, Jung felt the "negroid" attributes of the American soul were obvious, for instance, their laugh. One could best observe this by perusing the society gossip pages of American newspapers, he explained, and the "inimitable Roosevelt laugh" could be observed in its prototypical form in the "American Negro." The hip-swinging gait of American women supposedly also came from the "Negroes," and especially with respect to music and dance, "their dance is 'Negro' dance." Jung continued that the same was true for the naiveté and childishness of Americans and their unusually lively temperaments and "endless chatter." All of this could hardly be "traced back to Germanic ancestors, and much more resembles the chattering of a Negro village."[166]

The transition from traditional anti-American writing to ideologically tempered anti-Americanism, as would become commonplace in Nazism, can be identified in the conspiracy syndrome that depicted America as the product of Jewish rule per se. Otto Bonhard wrote a polemic in 1927 with the revealing title *Jüdische Weltherrschaft?* (Jewish World Domination?). It promoted a simple theory: America, striving toward world domination, represented a mere masquerade of the Jews. In his opinion, "Americanism" basically meant nothing more than Jewish thought and sentiment. This was primarily expressed in a specific form of "imperialism."[167] Another author, Alexander Graf Brockdorff, posed the rhetorical question of American world domination two years later in a work so titled. In happy anticipation he announced that the United States had little prospects for success, especially since the country was degenerating. It was the Jews who were primarily to blame for the degeneration, he continued, for American civilization was hopelessly at their mercy. There the "Jewish trend toward decline and demoralization" encountered far less established traditions; to that extent it was much easier in America "to destroy the [weak] sense of honor than it was in Europe." In particular, the democratic forms of state that prevailed in the United States furthered corruption and thus the Jews.[168]

Degeneration through modernity—that was the basic message of anti-Americanism. The hybridization of that which was supposedly naturally pure was introduced as a factor of degeneration. Halfeld, for example, described the way the American lifestyle eroded the "mythical foundation of (European) lineages that developed according to ethnic features" as threatening and culturally destructive. He wondered what Europe and America have in common that melts the Japanese and the Germans, the British and the Negroes into an "abstract, accidental national people"? He used natural images reminiscent of Nikolaus Lenau's melody a century earlier about the artificiality and mechanization of America—"no nightingales." Halfeld lamented that California fruit growers had succeeded in increasing the size of pineapples, melons, and grapefruits far beyond their natural growth—but at what cost! They took away the "aroma and taste that was a gift from heaven. And it is like that everywhere in this utilitarian culture."[169]

A successful author, Halfeld considered the emotional world of Americans emptied of all naturalness, as if dead. He saw jazz as symptomatic of such a world. Its vulgar, loud, crude, and hysterical syncopation supposedly revealed a feeling for life that had been denied existence by the puritanical repression of the senses and was now violently screaming for revolt. "Just as prohibition and jazz—

both born of war—existed parallel to each other, so must this new joviality necessarily be extravagant, since it is psychologically nothing but a reaction. It is the cocky merriness of the upstart nation. The American gospel of work and success was hardly acquainted with pure cosmopolitan happiness, and jazz is also foreign to it, a mere surrogate of emotion—socially acceptable barbarism and stimulated propaganda, displaying only inner emptiness and abandonment."[170] Graf Brockdorff totally agreed with such conclusions. The defects in the "American national character" culminated in contemptible "shallowness"[171]—a diagnosis which, incidentally, suited liberal minds as well.[172]

The stereotype of an America lacking in culture was obviously not an invention of the Weimar period, but represented the perpetuation of a tradition going back to the Romantics.[173] This stereotype was internalized to such an extent that even America enthusiasts made use of its images, including Alfred Kerr in his 1925 anthem for America, *Yankee Land*. There are passages in this travelogue in which the "childlike and youthful soul" of supposedly superficial Americans succumbs to the temptations of baseball, jazz, bobbed hair, film, and oil deposits.[174] Kerr is pro-American and, in light of German disappointment in America after Wilson's peace plan failed, his report should be seen as a type of well-meaning lesson to the Germans.[175] The mere fact that even such an author could not avoid using these kinds of stereotype clearly shows the depth of their impact.

Cast in a different mold is the 1930 report by Egon Erwin Kisch called *Paradies Amerika* (Paradise America). Kisch saw America not as one country among many, but as the metropolis of the capitalistic Moloch. There he encountered all that was expected, since his primary motivation was to describe the industrialism and Fordism that flattened out everything. It is conspicuous how star reporter

Kisch departed from his usual style when metaphorically describing the alienation; his wording complied totally with the common prejudices, beyond any justifiable social criticism. In a caricature presentation of Chicago, the people are stereotypically portrayed as monad-like, wandering through the metropolis blindly and without direction, pushing each other just "so a few millionaires from New York and Miami Beach, Florida can pocket another billion."[176]

It is no secret that Bertolt Brecht used America as the social backdrop for his literary social criticism of capitalism. It is not clear to what extent "America" stood solely for a compromised social order and thus for a distorted "projection of the current German situation,"[177] or whether a traditional hostility toward modernity slipped into his presentation of America.

Brecht's work is generally credited with an ambivalence toward America that is truly in keeping with the spirit of the times. Originally, he shared the pro-modern enthusiam for America that reached its climax in Germany around 1924-1926. Later his motivations reversed course. In November 1927 he was still reserved, yet positive, in his judgment of America; in 1930, the beginning of the Great Depression, when he wrote his poem *"Verschollener Ruhm der Riesenstadt New York"* (The Late Lamented Fame of the Giant City of New York), he had already completely changed his views and opposed the United States.[178] In *Aufstieg und Fall der Stadt Mahagonny* (The Rise and Fall of the City of Mahagonny), this trend was established once and for all.[179] America and capitalism became interchangeable metaphors—and the Soviet Union appeared as an optimistic counter-world. This contrast is dramatically expressed in the play via horror stories of daily events in capitalism played over a loudspeaker, in order to let the alternative appear at the same time: "The five-year plan in four

years!"[180] It is doubtful whether Brecht's left-wing criticism
of America in the 1920s would have been so sweeping
without the hopeful prospects of socialism and the Soviet
Union. In any case he later formulated his principle of
partisanship in no uncertain terms: "The mistakes of the
Russians are the mistakes of friends; the mistakes of the
Americans are the mistakes of enemies."

Even back then the similarity of left- and right-wing
images of America could have given people cause for concern. Kisch's America book, for example, received unani-
mous praise from the bourgeois press.[181] The "traveling reporter" spoke of "busy idleness" in America, where something was always being done and nothing really happened, i.e., people were very hard-working and busy, but
no work was accomplished.[182] This appraisal is not all that
different from the reactionary Graf Keyserling, who denied
American efficiency and "creativity" as follows: They
know "about work, but not about the product of that
labor."[183]

Although social criticism of America from the Left was
largely justified, the images they used hardly differed from
those used by the Right, which at its core was anti-modern
and pessimistic about civilization. The impact of the Right
was much more far-reaching because of their irrational explanations. Adolf Halfeld reduced the collective aversion
to America to a common denominator: "If we Germans
adopt an American way of thinking, then Greek civilization was for nothing, German mysticism was on the wrong
track, and the German Faustian soul is merely a personal
opinion of the late Goethe. America is killing Eros for the
sake of human machines."[184]

Weimar was filled with contradictions with respect to
America. Amidst "Americanization" in the economy, technology, and culture, the period was infected with spreading anti-Americanism. To that extent, the Weimar Republic

became a breeding ground for the same anti-American mentality in Germany whose traces can be followed to the present day.

Uncle Sam is Uncle Shylock

THE NAZI PREDICAMENT

"For the Freedom of all people: You can say what you want but this is
my war, which you should win for me."
Lustige Blätter, 1941

If it can be said that the political culture of the Weimar
Period was characterized by an ambivalent relationship to
America—blind enthusiasm as well as ideological hostility—then it can also be said that unambiguous rejection of
the United States spread during the Nazi Period. A text
published in 1943 clearly demonstrated the Nazis' negative
image of America by declaring that America stood for "the
countenance of a land and a people that murdered hun-
dreds of thousands of Indians to make room for themselves; that robbed other states of their rightful possessions
with lies and deception, violence and war; that occupied
other countries and subjugated peoples, casting them into
misery and exploiting their labor; that broke every promise
and every treaty standing in the way of its power and its
whims. It is the countenance of selfish, materialistic Anglo-
Saxons, convinced that God reserved the world for them to
rule, so they can do whatever they will with impunity! Like
a kraken, that many-armed beast of the ocean, this land
stretches its arms in all directions, grasping hold of islands,
countries, and peoples and suffocating them in its embrace.
Yet behind this monster appears the grotesque face of the
wandering Jew, who sees it as nothing less than a precur-
sor to the implementation of his ancient and never-aban-
doned plans to rule the world."[185] This torrent of accusato-
ry words projecting America as the epitome of Jewish
wheelings and dealings was in keeping with Hitler's view
of the world. According to Ernst "Putzi" Hanfstaengel,
Hitler's advisor on American affairs, Hitler originally paid
little attention to the United States as an independent fac-

tor, considering it instead merely one aspect of the "Jewish Question."[186] However, this view led to Hitler's unshakeable conviction of the supposed weakness of the United States. The German Foreign Office summarized the attitude of the "Führer" in a report as follows: "Hitler wanted to see an America unable to wage war, in the control of the Jews, facing social catastrophe, and D.N.B. [the German news agency] brought reports that made America appear this way."[187] Occasionally America received praise, but only in questions of racial politics, for example, when it was bemoaned that German or "species-similar blood" existed there that was being lost through genetic mixing. Other than that, Hitler's statements on the United States essentially brought together all the traditionally significant images and metaphors directed against America. In mid-1933, for example, Hitler made fierce derogatory comments about the Roosevelt administration, which had taken office a few months earlier.[188] According to Hitler, it represented the "last revolting death throes of an outmoded, corrupt system." Despite initial restraint, this became the tenor of all the regime's ideological commentary on the United States.

The Nazis faced a dilemma in their prejudice against America. Ideologically, America was seen as the incarnation of all that is degenerate. Politically, Hitler wanted nothing more than to keep the United States away from the European continent, and he therefore avoided any possible conflict. Evasion was accomplished through adroit manipulation of the press. It was possible to preserve this staged restraint, despite some turmoil, until 1938/39. Thereafter, the mask fell. Starting in 1940, i.e., before the United States entered the war, America and above all President Roosevelt were portrayed as the arch enemies of the world. Anti-Americanism was employed more and more as an ideological weapon. The wealth of well-researched texts and the large number of publications in the 1940s clearly show how much effort had been necessary for Goebbels to steer the press up till then, in order to hold back stored up hostility toward America. After all reserve had been abandoned, hostile feelings for the United States were given free rein. The anti-American publications that appeared after 1941 could not be considered merely propagandistic inventions resulting from the fact that the United States had entered the war. For many authors it represented a long-awaited opportunity.

Hitler also expressed his anti-Americanism openly and without fear of political repercussions, as follows: It is "... a decayed country, with problems of race and social inequality, of no ideas. . . . My feelings against America are those of hatred and repugnance; half Judaized, half negrified with everything built on the dollar. . . . Americans. . . have the brains of a hen. The country is a house of cards with an uneven material level. Americans live like sows, though. . . in a most luxurious sty."[189]

Such an invective is very much a part of the tradition of pre-Nazi anti-Americanism. Despite Hitler's fascination with the technically advanced—modern—aspects of American civilization, such as his interest in its architecture or the mass production in the automobile industry (the Volkswagen was supposed to be an ambitious copy of Ford, and its mass motorization a means to level out class differences), he considered life in the United States condemned to failure and consumed by decadence. His characterization of America contained many elements of conservative, aristocratic, and anti-egalitarian traditions: "Ever since the Civil War, in which the southern states lost, contrary to all historical logic and common sense, the Americans are now in a stage of political and national decay." Not only had the southern states been defeated; the American people themselves, in his eyes, had suffered a terrible defeat. The eco-

nomic and political rise achieved by the United States nevertheless thus represented a mere illusory boom. In reality,
after the Civil War, America "was caught up in the turmoil
of progressive self-destruction." A merchant caste tri-
umphed over a "true master class." The social order based
on slavery and inequality that had cast away those false
ideas of liberty and equality had been destroyed. Meanwhile, a kind of "equality" had taken hold that made no
distinctions between descendents of old Spanish aristocracy, Swedish settlers, and "the degenerate masses from Po-
land, Bohemia, Hungary, the entire scum of Eastern European Jewry and the Balkans. . ." But the fate of America
was by no means sealed. Hitler himself felt a calling "to
free the American people from their ruling clique and give
them the chance to become a great nation." On the other
hand, he felt the forces to blame for the decline of the
racially aristocratic America were represented by the Jews.
As he had diagnosed in *Mein Kampf*, "Jews are the regents
to the stock market giants of the American union."[190]

In the extensive and widely circulated anti-American
literature of the Nazis, Jewish forces of evil and corruption
colluded with a supposedly anti-German east coast aristocracy of British descent. In league with the Jews, this aristocracy was guilty of treason against the positive values of
the original America. After all, America did not enter the
war of its own free will; instead, the United States was
dragged into the war against the Reich by Germany's hated enemy, England, and its slavishly obedient cronies on
the east coast. That, at least, was the theory expounded on
a broad scale in Nazi-oriented writing after 1941. None of
this was new to Hitler himself. In disparaging monologues
in his headquarters, he maintained that the Americans did
not have a great future ahead of them, for the simple reason that, in his view, they were "a depraved and corrupt
state." To that extent, the military might of the Americans

need not be feared. Echoing the German military's traditional contempt for America, Hitler boasted of the supposed military incompetence of the United States. "The
American is no soldier. The inferiority and decadence of
the allegedly new world is evident in its military ineffi-
ciency."[191] In 1941 he told Japanese ambassador Oshima
that American military strength in 1918 was only mediocre.
"How could troops whose God is the dollar, hold firm to
the last?"[192]

Even all of these stories combined fail to depict the
Third Reich's entire image of America. Hitler's fascination
with technology alone reveals other, so-to-speak opposing
factors. Contrary to other portrayals, mostly in older writings on the position of National Socialist Germany toward
America, certain characteristics of the American lifestyle
occasionally met with approval in the Third Reich and
even prompted imitations. These, however, were limited
mostly to practical efficiency and modernization, production and manufacturing, and party- and state-fostered
measures to de-individualize daily life and eliminate class-
based differences in lifestyles. In short, trends were promoted that accelerated the pace of daily life, such as the
state-fostered modernistic worship of the automobile and
airplane. The only aspects of the American model to be em-
ulated in Germany of the 1930s were those relating to technology and "mass culture." In this respect, Nazi Germany
could be regarded as striving to be "modern" and "American." Author Hans Dieter Schäfer referred to the apparently paradoxical circumstance in the 1930s that, behind a veil
of propaganda opposing "liberalistic American selfish-
ness" and the "rule of the machine," attempts were made
to follow U.S. American development and its technical culture. Thus while visiting the United States in 1936, the con-
structor Ferdinand Porsche studied the Ford plant in De-
troit, preparing to introduce mass production of the Volk-

swagen. In retrospect, it also seems surprising that the walls of the Sport Palace were emblazoned with an advertisement to drink "ice-cold Coca-Cola."[193] Much in keeping with the Americanism popular during the Weimar period, a wealth of literature on America appeared during the prewar years of the Third Reich that painted a very well-meaning, almost idealized picture of the United States.[194]

Even in the political sphere, the Nazis' stance toward America was ambivalent, largely for clearly tactical reasons. The regime attempted to justify the initial political restraint it had shown the United States by arguing that President Roosevelt should not be given a reason to abandon the neutrality that Congress had adopted. The instructions of the Propaganda Ministry to the press in the 1930s had the effect of protecting the United States and its president. Under no circumstances were those on the other side of the Atlantic to get the impression Germany was anti-American. Even comments approving American restraint in the European conflict were discouraged. The instructions to the press prescribed that it was better to write nothing at all than to fuel the argument that Roosevelt's opposition was playing up to Germany.[195] Opponents of Roosevelt's policy within the United States tended to be more in favor of taking increased responsibility in international affairs, and the Nazis did not want them compromised by comparisons. It was understandably the strategic interest of the Third Reich to support promoters of isolationism in the United States who spoke passionately of "Fortress America" and hoped to keep America from becoming actively involved in politics on the European continent. Under no circumstances was the United States to be challenged to interfere in German plans for change and later expansion in Europe. [196]

This restraint applied mostly to foreign policy. Ideologically the Nazis made no secret of the fact that they believed American lifestyles to be profoundly degenerate. Appropriate measures were taken in the cultural sphere. Jazz and swing music, already frowned upon in any case as "Jewish and nigger frivolity," were outlawed outright in 1935. Such prohibitions hardly detracted from the popularity of these rhythms. Despite all adversity, they continued to enjoy a widespread following.[197] This can very well be interpreted as subtle, apolitical resistance to the far-reaching control of everyday life. The regime in turn remained flexible enough to avoid a head-on confrontation with simple pleasures in times of hardship. Although official propaganda continued to polemicize against "alien Americanism," and insisted on the incompatibility of "jazz and uniforms," fans of "weird music" in the Wehrmacht were no longer reprimanded. But the opposite was also true, for example, the threat in 1942 of being sent to a concentration camp for spreading "anglophile trends."[198]

Despite their leniency in small things, the Nazis meant business in their fight against what they considered decadent and degenerate pro-American trends. In a brochure on the dangers of "Americanism" published in 1944 by the office of the "Reichsführer SS," jazz was characterized as a Jewish weapon "to forcibly create a perfect international human community," an instrument of unrestrained liberalism. "The overall atmosphere, susceptible to jazz, is that of a levelling out of all national and racial differences, as liberalism has done throughout the world."[199]

Two tendencies can be observed with respect to the Third Reich: Americanism that developed naturally in the culture of daily life and in the supposedly non-ideological areas of technical innovation and modernization, on the one hand, and ideologically motivated anti-Americanism, on the other. This drew on deeper and older traditions—some of them stemming from the Weimar period—that merely needed to be revived. Concessions were made, to a certain extent, to audiences' preference for American films and music. But it seems greatly exaggerated to view such modernisms of the Third Reich as specific—German— forms of Americanism. The opposite is more likely the case; that is, the Third Reich was largely just what it claimed to be: anti-Western in a very traditional sense, antisemitic in terms of racial ideology, and anti-American to the extent that elements of American culture pertaining to everyday life, politics, and civilization were radically rejected.

Despite the adaptation of "technical" America—and this definitely came in the wake of Weimar developments—National Socialism perceived its ideology and identified itself as *the* ideological counterpart per se to the United States. It is dubious to argue that Nazism pushed forward German modernization and that Hitler aimed to make Germany into a "second America." Just as dubious is the notion that a "successful struggle against the property and privilege of the upper classes" had been waged and the "supremacy of nobility and aristocracy" broken, in the sense of evening out the social classes in the population.[200] Such arguments do not compare Hitler with the technically modern United States as much as they lump the United States together with a war-mongering and imperialistic Hitler. Such claims of convergence come dangerously close to the theory of "Roosevelt's imperialist war," widespread in revisionist historical literature. According to this theory, the only reason the United States entered World War II was its reluctance to abandon "its expansive trade policies. The more Hitler succeeded in damming the American flood, as called for by Wilhelm II, and keeping U. S. companies out of the southeastern European and Latin American markets, the more willing the United States would have been to defend its economic interests militarily."[201] There was indeed a contrast developing between Nazi ideas of autarchy and the bilateralist, anti–global market foreign trade politics of Hjalmar Schacht, on the one hand, and America's "open door" free trade ideas, on the other, but presenting this conflict as the real reason Roosevelt's America entered the war is much more than a reduction of history to sheer economism. The fact is, in the end the United States was, as a means of social critique, placed on a par with Nazism. Schäfer himself offered proof, reasoning that the methods of the Nazi regime were "a modern system of government based on the American model, which allows the democracies of post-bourgeois society to continue to exercise domination and try to perpetuate its technocratic system."[202]

Such a judgment reverses historical causality in revisionist fashion. According to this, it was not Hitler and the Third Reich that caused the catastrophe of the Second World War, but an abstract context of civilization, with the United States at the helm, even after the decline of the "Thousand Year Reich." This reversal was, incidentally, by no means atypical for the political culture of the Federal Republic of Germany. The crimes of the Nazis were instead blamed on America, psychological transference, so to speak, but more on that later.

At the beginning of the war, anti-American literature began to appear like a spring tide. This included malicious works such as Giselher Wirsing's *Der maßlose Kontinent* (The Excessive Continent) and A.E. Johann's *Land ohne Herz* (Land without a Heart), to name only the most significant ones. Such writings also appeared, however, in the period leading up to the war.[203]

In his Reichstag speech in April 1939, it was the "Führer" himself who broke with the restraint that had been shown the United States up till then. Hitler's attacks on the American president came during the "defeat" of "the remainder of Czechoslovakia." He mockingly rejected Roosevelt's offer of peace and, analogous to the American

Monroe Doctrine of 1823, demanded that "intervention by
powers alien to the territory be prohibited" in Europe. This
was the same view articulated in a speech held a short time
earlier by Carl Schmitt, the leading constitutional and international lawyer of the Reich. In a certain sense Hitler
thus claimed global parity with America.

Hitler's anti-Americanism is interesting for the bio-
graphical touch with which he contrasted himself and Germany to Roosevelt and America. He dramatically emphasized that "Roosevelt was rich, I was poor; Roosevelt did
business in the world war, I bled; Roosevelt speculated and
made millions, I lay in a hospital. Roosevelt relied on the
power of a capitalist party, I led a popular movement."[204]
Roosevelt thus seemed a reincarnation of the hated Wilson.
At a special press conference called on 15 April 1939, the
following remarks were made: "Second Wilson. . . the
number one warmonger. . . [who] wants to make the world
happy after he has produced an unparalleled war psy-
chosis."[205] The United States even attacked the German
Empire in 1917 "without any pressing justification . . .
merely for capitalist reasons."[206]

Direct comparisons with the First World War also led to
the Atlantic Charter, drawn up by Roosevelt and Churchill
in August 1941 on the battleship Augusta off the coast
of Newfoundland, as well as the "Four Freedoms," announced a few months earlier, which were supposed to
serve as the foundation for a new, liberal world order after
the war. In Goebbels's August 15th diary entry, he directly
took up where the Wilson-hatred of the postwar period left
off, denouncing values tied to freedom and free trade as
pure hypocrisy, "This propaganda bluff is summarized in
eight points, a new Wilson proclamation, so to speak. The
contents of these eight points is the oldest inventory of
democratic propaganda."[207] Now even the very last remnants of a positive appraisal of America had been aban-

doned, to be replaced by horror propaganda in which the United States functioned as a stronghold of capitalist exploitation, breeding ground for misery and "gangsters, cheap sensation-seekers, lack of culture, and self-destructiveness." There wasn't much new in this, as these clichés had long since become familiar and popular. "The propaganda was able to borrow old prejudices, in part from nineteenth century traditions, taking up remembered criticism of America from the 1920s and early 1930s."[208] These were supplemented by descriptions of the misery of the Great Depression and—of course—well-honed and intensified racist ideology.

The abovementioned book by Giselher Wirsing, *Der maßlose Kontinent*, illustrates the way in which anti-Americanism gained the upper hand during the war. This book is exemplary of the arsenal of anti-American polemics in the Third Reich in that it confuses an expertise on the subject that would be extraordinary for Germany with wild ideological distortions. This mixture constitutes an ideologically structured lie employing empirical truths. The author made a name for himself as a well-traveled journalist. His books enjoyed a large circulation and found a place on the bookshelves of the educated class. Wirsing was particularly interested in waging a journalistic campaign against "Anglo-Saxon imperialism," especially that of the United States. Before German-American relations worsened, this judgment seemed to be reserved for England alone. Wirsing knowledgeably denounced British politics in the Near East and the colonies as the wheelings and dealings of "perfidious Albion," while at the same time extolling Germany as the natural ally of the peoples enslaved by colonialism. Wirsing's career did not end with the war. In the early years of the Federal Republic, one of the positions held by the former high-ranking SS man was the prominant job of editor in chief of the weekly, *Christ und Welt*.

Wirsing knew how to tie his current events approach to the ways of the world into a historical framework. He interpreted the two times the United States entered a war, 1917 and 1941, as necessary expressions of a deep structural crisis faced by America when the continental expansion process was concluded at the end of the nineteenth century. The "frontier" had come to a natural end. Taking up the theory of H.J. Turner, he saw the expansion overseas, especially in the Pacific region, as a necessary consequence, as it were, of the American way of life.

This hypothesis that imperialist expansion became a mere nececessity for the United States starting in 1898, the year of the Spanish-American War, found acceptance among various historians; even in the United States, it had more than just a few followers. Wirsing took this derivation to its radical extreme when he wrote that the goal of American expansion was nothing more nor less than "world domination."[209] The author's perspective stood out in that it referred primarily to smaller schemes by individuals and interest groups, machinations and intrigues by cliques working in secret. He reduced politics in general to plotting and conspiracy, referring to great American "financial pirates" of the late 19th century who formed an all-controlling "plutocracy" intending to implement a joint, imperialistic program. In Wirsing's opinion, the Puritan-Calvinist ideology, according to which earthly success was a sign of God's grace, helped big business hide its evil deeds beneath a religious veil. With such moral exculpation, only minimal effort was required to take over the state. "And the State Department . . . is essentially the great agent of finance capital, using state means of power diplomatically and militarily for the financial interests of the various ruling economic groups." The Marines, who turn up particularly in the Caribbean and Central America, were the executors of the great plans of high finance.[210]

And this supposedly led directly to American loan policies in Europe after the world war, in which the United States boasted its new role as "world creditor." Wirsing alluded to the different moods common at the time of the debate on the Dawes Plan. "If up to now it had been Cuba, Haiti, Santo Domingo, and Nicaragua where American ambassadors served as executors of the wishes of Wall Street, this time it was the German Empire, beaten into the ground, in which the so-called 'reparations agents'—Dawes, Young, and Perker-Gilbert—appeared as representatives of the J.P. Morgan banking house, authorized by the American government. However, they headed the tribute commissions— the last of which would have obligated Germany to make tribute payments until 1988—not as official representatives of the government, but as 'simple American citizens.'"[211]

The particularly reprehensible, imperialist form of indirect rule was described as it had been back in the Weimar period, as typically American. Whereas other peoples acted openly and above board in a genuine struggle for survival, the United States supposedly veiled its interests in principles and doctrines, which it tried to impose on others as the "American way of life." Wirsing was able to list twenty-four instances of North American intervention between 1823 and 1941 undertaken in the name of "dollar imperialism" and "Yankee imperialism."[212] The corruption that America brought to the world like a hydra, according to Wirsing, was based in the propagation and exploitation of allegedly universal principles that served only its own, absolutely selfish interests.

And, of course, these hypocritical principles were clothed in doctrines of international law that actually served only the mighty or the agents of the status quo. This is why Wirsing vehemently polemicized against the U.S. Stimson Doctrine of 1932. After Japan occupied Manchuria, America declared any and all one-sided territorial changes to be illegal, and any such action was opposed on principle. Later revisions, annexations, and other conquests by Nazi Germany also fell unter this rubric. Wirsing indignantly rejected such American presumptuousness. "Even now the State Department still thinks there is a 'Free State of Danzig,' a Czechoslovakia, etc." For Wirsing, the Stimson Doctrine thus represented the transition of the United States from imperialist isolationism after World War I to a new form of expansionist imperialism.[213]

Wirsing heaped scorn on the Kellogg-Briand Pact, negotiated in 1927 primarily by the United States, which renounced war per se. In the American, pacifist tradition of international law, this condemned war as an "instrument of national politics." In Wirsing's opinion it thus served only those who worked to maintain the order imposed by Versailles.[214] Referring to Carl Schmitt, Wirsing mocked the distinction made in the Kellogg-Briand Pact between wars "designated as 'just' by a kind of international allied action," and those which are not. "In other words, the Kellogg-Briand Pact was an attempt by American imperialism, allied with the French and British varieties, to decide which wars should be allowed and which should not, which wars should be opposed, and which could be waged as morally justified."[215] The longevity of such argumental structures became obvious during the 1991 Gulf War. This discourse was not carried on as knowledgeably as on the right-wing intellectual fringes,[216] yet traces could be found everywhere.

In determining significant details of American imperialism, Giselher Wirsing uses images and lines of argumentation that were typical of both the extreme right wing and the National-Bolshevist extreme Left during the Weimar Republic. However, a remarkable intensification can be observed, leading to a closed global interpretation. Wirsing suggested that a very special plan to rule the world was lurking behind the new expansionist phase of the American imperialism he condemned: the Jews were using the development of American power to set themselves up as the rulers of the world. Even before the Nazi period, anti-Semitism and anti-Americanism converged through images and metaphors that were similar at least in structure. But what was once only vaguely implied now underwent a semiofficial unveiling. Wirsing hit upon an image for an ideological prejudice that was crystalizing, by frankly declaring that "Uncle Sam has been transformed into Uncle Shylock."[217]

There were good tactical reasons to denounce America as a materialistic, "excessive continent" enslaved by Jewish domination. Even Hitler had not totally given up America for lost, and had counted on the "healthy forces" in the country. This required distinguishing between the "true" America and the rule of finance capital that could be traced back to Jewish wheelings and dealings. In opposition to this financial strength, "another" America was to emerge.

German propaganda then started targetting what it considered the corrupting forces, a plutocracy that worked in the shadows and forced America to enter the war against Germany against its will. "Jewish warmongers" were joined after 1940 by anglophile upper classes on the American east coast. This argument was used primarily by Adolf Halfeld, already cited several times. In 1941 he joined the fray again, this time with an interesting theory on the question of responsibility for the war. His hypothesis was that both camps on Wall Street were conspiring against Germany—"the old 'English' houses and an equally powerful Jewish group led by the banking firms of Kuhn, Loeb & Co., Lehman Brothers, and James Speyer, the Lewinsohn and Guggenheim interests." It was the "upper ten thousand, high finance, and even the intellectual elites of the United States; in short, the English party of the country," with whose support Great Britain was pushing the United States into the war.[218] They were committing nothing less than treason against America's independence, according to Halfeld. The declaration of independence from England in 1776 and the Monroe Doctrine—with its dissociation from Europe—were thereby nullified. An English infiltration of the United States was taking place, Halfeld continued, and Roosevelt was only able to achieve support for the war by using demogogical slogans, according to which America had to defend itself in Great Britain. Although it was hardly a desire of all thinking Americans that the seas be ruled solely by the English-speaking nations, Halfeld's claim was certainly characteristic of the influential and wealthy classes, which felt very rooted to the English nature from time immemorial.[219] But that was not all: "Even today, some citizens of the United States have loyalist attitudes lying dormant. We spoke of the English party of the wealthy ruling class. It, however, does not represent the common people."[220]

The difference between the true, good America, such as the farmers of the midwest, and the corruptible combination of Jews, intellectuals, and high finance, with its incestuous ties to England, was represented by no one better than Franklin D. Roosevelt. Halfeld used a remarkable political topography to describe how such an alliance came into being. Of all presidents since the end of the Civil War, only two were native-born New Yorkers: Theodore and Franklin D. Roosevelt. This remark is significant, since the point was to emphasize the implied antithesis of the good and well-mannered America of the northern European immigrants and the disastrous ethnic jumble of people in the city of New York. Even the early east coast immigrants were a mixture of people with English, Scottish, German, and Dutch backgrounds. And they who explored the West were pioneers of the same race—essentially Germans and

Scandinavians. "And it is their descendants who feel connected to the continent with heart and soul and who, very early on, saw the purely profit-oriented and speculative business of later immigrants—very often of other races and many Jewish elements—as foreign and contrary to tradition." These "alien elements" settled in the metropolis on the Hudson and gained the upper hand there. *"Neuyork alone has about three million Jewish residents, and others will follow who as well do not belong to the original stock. It is obvious that particular kinds of political and social problems will arise through this peculiar social composition."*[221]

Halfeld was of the opinion that "the Jew" held sway in America. "The Jew's" ethnic and social qualities predestined him for such rule, allowing him to adapt far more easily to the American lifestyle than "any other type of breed." He had little to lose—but everything to win, especially since "his calculating mind" was suited in every way to the "functional culture of the New World, the dance around the golden calf, and the ethics of success of North Americans." He felt comfortable, since the country lacked long-standing traditions and did not mistrust him from the start. "He learned English easily, since the Yiddish tongue, the language of his ghetto, meant little to him. North America was the perfect elixir of life for his type."[222]

Halfeld's ethnopsychological theories did not merely portray the Jews as a particular group with a special interest in pushing out the original Nordic stock in the midwest. A habitual hatred of Germans was also ascribed to them. According to Halfeld, it was the Jews who forced the United States to enter the war. The picture was finally complete: the Jews stood for everything connected with "America" that had to do with alienation and the expression of modernity. "The Jew" of the United States was considered "the sum of all American civic virtues, for even the foundation of his ascension was the ideal of the equality of all people. He thought—doubtless with inner conviction—of the United States as the earthly homeland of his cosmopolitanism. For him, human rights were the gospel of the North American people, the message that he was supposed to proclaim to all peoples. From this perspective, it seemed un-American for people clinging to the soil of their forebears to take up the cause of the peace and self-sufficiency of their wealthy continent."[223] The writer raised himself to the status of a Nazi historical philosopher and, in a very unoriginal, albeit eloquent, manner, he set universalism against isolationism—for him, a battle between the Jewish cosmopolitan ideal and the German principle of blood and soil. Although a member of one of the oldest families in the country, Roosevelt—according to Halfeld—owed his public success to those circles "that kept the wheels of the Democratic Party machine in New York turning." Halfeld found it by no means surprising that the Roosevelt Era saw the rise in influence of such men as New York mayor Fiorello LaGuardia, Viennese-born professor Felix Frankfurter, "and the son of the anti-German wartime ambassador, Secretary of the Treasury Henry Morgenthau, who had family ties to the great international New York banking firms of Kuhn, Loeb & Co., Lewinsohn, and Seligman."[224] The consequences of this situation were catastrophic and would have been unthinkable had America been ruled by the long-established, hard-working Nordic residents of the good old American midwest. "Niggers received in the White House—Jews in the highest positions of government—the population of the metropolis on the Hudson, whose original stock has been simply flooded by the sea of foreign blood—and equality of all humanity as the wide cloak that is supposed to lovingly cover it all."[225]

Such an ethnification of politics was in the end a rationalization of discomfort that American reactions to Hitler's politics were becoming increasingly hostile. Roosevelt could indeed easily be mentioned in connection with "Jewish interests"—he did become infuriated at the treatment of Jews in the Reich, and despite any opportunistic restraint, he did not keep his opinions to himself. He recalled the head of the U.S. mission in Berlin in protest at the pogrom in November 1938, the so-called Kristallnacht. With that move, Roosevelt revealed himself in the eyes of the Nazis as a friend of Jews and enemy of Germany. The Nazis' self-imposed restraint toward America was abandoned for a time, and an intense propaganda campaign against Roosevelt was triggered. Totally in keeping with its antisemitic world view, the Nazi newspaper *Völkischer Beobachter* denounced the American president as nothing but a henchman of Jewish power in the United States. It was insinuated that Roosevelt expressed his displeasure only because he was serving not American interests, but sinister, supranational ones. "The greatest of these wretched powers is world Jewry." The *Völkischer Beobachter* ran the following headline: "World Jewry ['Alljuda'] awards Roosevelt the medal of the Hebrews." The same tabloid offered another informative headline in early 1939: "USA under Jewish dictatorship."[226]

The subject of Jewish rule in America needed an in-depth explanation. Giselher Wirsing reported that in the early expansionist period of American imperialism, the era of Teddy Roosevelt—the one with the "big stick"—relatively few Jews were found on the face of America. The world war favored them to such an extent that they were able to "penetrate" the financial oligarchy.[227] Once FDR became president—and he was soon accused of having Jews in the family—the Jews were said to have finally taken control of America. According to Wirsing, it was incontestable that there were Jewish "relatives in one branch of the Roosevelt family," that is, Eleanor Roosevelt's—her mother was supposedly "the Jewess or half-Jewess Rebekka Hall."[228]

But if anyone were anti-German in America it was its Jews, who had long been actively working to ruin Germany. Bernard Baruch, Wilson's secretary of finance, was mentioned again and again in this context. He was an advisor in 1919/1920 to then-president Wilson at the Paris Peace Conferences. "Baruch was often the sole delegate to the consultations of the 'Big Four.' The financial provisions of the Versailles Treaty that would bleed Germany were essentially his work. The Dawes Plan, which enslaved Germany's wealth to the hilt, was also drafted mainly by Baruch. We can see how, once again, one of the authors of the Versailles Treaty, and on top of that one of the most powerful members of Roosevelt's New York financial Jewry, was given an active role at a decisive point in history."[229]

A key figure used in depicting supposed Jewish influence was the aforementioned law professor and Roosevelt confidante, Felix Frankfurter. According to Wirsing's scenario, Frankfurter strove for nothing less than secret control of the United States. He was successful in his intrigues, managing to fill numerous positions in the Roosevelt Administration with his mostly Jewish students. Acting in cahoots with the lodges (that is, the freemasons), whose influence could hardly be overestimated, they ensnared the president and administration.[230] In any case, there was enough evidence, wrote Wirsing, that the Frankfurters' drawing room was an important center of power and influence starting in 1917. That was where the secretaries of the most important government departments came from. Frankfurter's people held positions everywhere, said Wirsing, "and most of his people were Jews."[231]

With the reforms of the New Deal, also referred to disparagingly as the "Jew Deal," Frankfurter was supposedly able to increase his power. At first even the Nazis seemed

to find something positive about this project. They thought
they recognized parallels with their own economic and social policies. In any case, announcements in the Nazi-con-
trolled press first praised Roosevelt as a kind of dictatorial
führer. He supposedly possessed the stature of a "national
führer, a regent with unusual leadership qualities and the
power of a leader."[232] Although Americans still clung to the
illusion of democracy, the "development of an authoritarian state loomed on the horizon."[233] In one of the first reports on Roosevelt in June 1933, on the occasion of the publication of his book *Looking Forward*, an editorial in the
Völkische Beobachter obviously misinterpreted American
circumstances, commenting that the energetic president
had recognized the disastrous damage caused by unbridled individualism. "Some sentences could have been
written by a National Socialist. In any case, it can be assumed that Roosevelt has a great deal of understanding for
the thought processes of Nazism."[234] A critic for the *Berliner Tageblatt* discovered "planned economy ideas all over"
Roosevelt's publication.[235] In the early years of the Nazi period, Goebbels imploringly sought common ground between America and Germany. Both nations were supposedly caught in a heroic struggle for freedom against the terrible crisis of the times.[236] When the president's 1936 New
Year's message publicized the fact that under no circumstances would Roosevelt accept Germany's revisionist and
expansionist policies, opinions changed, even with respect
to the New Deal reforms. Roosevelt, previously chided as
the "pope of democracy," "Wilson's successor," and "world
umpire," was now the target of attacks in the area of domestic policy as well.[237] Critics claimed the American president failed in his economic and social policies, saying this
forced him to escape into foreign policy. This was accompanied by the checking of isolationist forces. According to
Halfeld, as in 1917 they were forced into the "background

by English and Jewish influence in the east."[238]

By the end of the 1930s, Nazi writings began declaring the New Deal an absolute failure. Any former praise of the reformist project had been forgotten. More and more, it was disparagingly revealed to be a dilettantish enterprise by "Jewish intellectual schools" (Wirsing). Robert Ley, director of the German Labor Front and responsible for social policy, spoke obscenely of "Jewish crap."[239] In the revised Nazi view, the New Deal had been doomed to failure from the very start.[240] The Jewish intelligentsia that Roosevelt recruited into government and administration were to blame. The failure of the whole project went to show "that the Jewish intelligentsia is not in the position to draft truly farsighted and innovative plans. They are merely able to analyze and invent short-term remedies. . . . The limitations set upon the Jewish intelligentsia by their shortage of true creativity are strikingly confirmed by the fiasco of the New Deal. A debate club cannot take the place of genius." This subtle homage to Hitler represented the final judgment.[241]

Wirsing considered Roosevelt a victim of Felix Frankfurter's whispered council, possible because of his intellectual dependence on Judaism. This weakness of the president was destined to "be a virtually ideal starting point for Judaism, to which he felt close ties since his early youth through the freemason lodges."[242] "In this way, high finance, Jewish intelligentsia, and communists" had conspired to ruin Germany.[243] The Roosevelt administration was thus a paradigm of the unity—according to the Nazis—of Judaism, plutocracy, and Bolshevism. But Nazism supposedly had little to fear from this combination, which was condemned to failure. "Judaism, which has become an outpost of Americanism everywhere it appears in the world, has found itself on the defensive even in places where it still prevails."[244]

Wirsing's ideas were passed off as visionary and extremely forward-looking. Salvation, in the form of National Socialism, had started its victory procession in Germany, one of the most powerful industrial nations in the world. National Socialism exerted an incredible power of attraction on all other peoples "at the mercy of the conflict between shortage and surplus." These peoples would realize at some time that the liberty they supposedly enjoyed "pertains only to the lifestyle of the monied oligarchy." The cure would come with the abandonment of the economic system connected with this liberty. As soon as the concept of liberty took on a socialist meaning the lamented rift between shortage and surplus would close. And how was this "possible within the Anglo-Saxon capitalist system?" Ultimately, through the inevitable hostility of these peoples toward the United States. Didn't Americanism "prove to be the opposite of National Socialism throughout the world?"[245]

Giselher Wirsing, anti-imperialist and national socialist, saw the conflict of the Second World War as a struggle between the Anglo-Saxon form of capitalist imperialism and an anti-colonial Nazism. Like other Nazi authors, Wirsing did not regard Bolshevism as truly socialist, since it was international. Rather, he felt it was the expression of merely one specific form of modernistic mass society and alienation of the individual—in short, Americanism.

"USA–SA–SS"

POST-WAR PROJECTIONS

"The only Germany the Yankee liked was one alienated from its true nature."[246]

Before the war was even over, Adolf Halfeld reduced German-American relations to this expression of false reconciliation. Germany's alienation from itself did indeed become a constant topic in anti-American discourse after 1945. According to this standpoint, Germans lost their authenticity and self-esteem through reeducation and imposed democracy. The Federal Republic was even considered an American creation, a mere economic and constitutional state, to be dealt with only for practical reasons.

Such a tenor could be observed in contemporary writing in a variety of genres. It was so general that it cut clear across the common political division between "left" and "right." It is characterized by a pronounced anti-American quality, even anti-Western, and its impact can still be felt today.

A review of anti-American sentiments and opinions from the early years of the Federal Republic of Germany proves that they have very much retained their relevance even now. This likely owes even more to the fact that German history is once again in a state of flux. Historical perspectives have found a new orientation; assessments are being re-thought, sometimes turning things around totally. What had once seemed everlasting is suddenly being reevaluated entirely. This applies especially to the fundamental question of Germany's self-image—its position toward the West.

For over forty years, the "West" stood for a politically

well-defined entity, that is, ideologically and in terms of power politics. The "West" was comprised of a system of alliances directed against another well-defined system: the "East." Such distinctions and their related interpretations have become not only dubious, but obsolete. They have simply ceased to exist. In their place, other long since outdated positions have reappeared. The old-new images and metaphors for interpreting Us and Them also use the points of the compass. Only the contents have changed. The "West" that is once again spoken of in a very different way than it was during the cold war, no longer stands opposite an ideologically clearly defined East. Rather, it is distinguished in terms of historical references and cultural, geographical spheres from, for example, central Europe. In any case, Germany does not really belong to the primarily political and cultural "West"—distinct from the political West of the East-West conflict—as represented by its core countries: the United States, England, France, and Holland. Whether the Germany that was newly unified in 1990 will intuitively consider itself part of the "West" and feel committed to that political culture in the future; whether the integration with the political and institutional West after 1945 has become so firmly rooted that this country can be regarded as Western even in a cultural sense, in order to evade the predicament owing to its central location and the temptation brought with that—this remains an anxious question for the future.

But what does all this have in common with anti-Americanism and its historical impact in the Federal Republic of Germany? Well, the stance toward America is an indicator for the westernization of Germany. This does not refer to any random critical or affirmative position regarding the respective administration, or this or that change in American politics, but the fundamental position toward the values and attitudes, lifestyles and value references considered to be an expression of American political culture. It is a matter of belonging to a context of "Western" civilization based on the foundation of individual freedom and democracy.

In the early postwar period, the western German zones could not reasonably be regarded as "Western" despite their political ties to the West. This was true, even though the public was thoroughly pro-American, in view of the Soviet threat and the establishment of a communist regime in the eastern part of the country. But the degree of acceptance of everything American back then is greatly overestimated in retrospect. Today, people sometimes even claim that Germany was overly identified with America in the postwar years. The Germans simply exchanged their over-identification with Hitler and the Nazis with an over-identification with America, according to some psychoanalysts. The authority was merely transferred to the victor, the United States. Horst-Eberhard Richter, for example, spoke of a "psychological Americanization reaching down to the very unconscious, which characterizes broad segments of our society." Just how problematic such a psychoanalytical presumption can be and the degree of hostility toward America that is projected by such a liberation psychology, becomes obvious in further explanations by the psychologist. He spoke of the "imported psyche"[247] of America and the opposing therapeutic goal of resisting it and "developing in us a new independent Germanness."[248]

America as a substitute for Hitler: Richter diagnosed a ubiquitous, uncritical, even obsequious pro-Americanism in Germany. In Richter's view this could be recognized in the submissive attitude of the West German government toward the successive U.S. administrations, particularly in the area of security policies.

Any psychological interpretation risks criticism as an indulgence in drawn-out speculation—in any case, its specific findings cannot be confirmed. Though a lot might support such an interpretation, just as much does not. Ultimately, whether or not it is convincing depends on its sheer plausibility and being part of a historical interpretation.

Definitive conclusions rarely follow even from a historical appraisal, however. Nevertheless, it is very doubtful whether the German population really showed sympathies toward America from the very beginning and if it was thus at all fitting to speak of their own self-perception being replaced by an outside, American influence, not to mention their being reeducated.

In any case, it is appropriate to doubt the popular finding of blind pro-Americanism. Just as Nazi propaganda against Americanism was only successful to the extent that it took advantage of anti-western hostilities that already existed, attitudes in the postwar period were impacted by the persisting, traditional ambivalence in attitudes toward America. After all, this had to do with long-standing, albeit up-dated, stereotypes. Anyway, there was no blind identification with the victor directly after the war. More likely, Germans faced Americans from a reserved and mockingly supercilious stance.

So, not a trace of joyful enthusiasm toward America. The mere fact of indiscriminate Allied area bombing bolstered existing hostilities toward the "Anglo-Saxons"; the term "Allies" seemed to apply exclusively to the British and the Americans. Nazi propaganda in the final months and weeks of the war also served to reinforce stereotypes in the German consciousness. Schemed rumors were a specialty of Goebbels, and so it was announced in 1944/45 that American "decrees for the enslavement of the German people" had been issued. Realistic-sounding reports were spread, such as the story that the civilian population was being "forced by nigger guards to do clean-up work in the line of German artillery fire"; German children were being lured by American chocolate and then kidnapped, and others "murdered by drunk niggers";[249] Aachen was under the knout of Eisenhower—"Jews and emigrants terrorizd the city—furniture and valuables confiscated—'Out of the way, you German swine!'" was the headline of the Limburg newspaper on October 30, 1944.[250]

The atmosphere of an impending ultimate judgment hardened into an image that contributed more than anything else in transferring anti-American and anti-Jewish hostilities from the Nazi period into the Federal Republic. It was the image of the man supposedly out to ruin Germany—Henry Morgenthau and the Morgenthau Plan.

This picture, carved into the collective consciousness, can be regarded as epitomizing the myths of the postwar period. This non-event served to confirm a view that not only saw Germany as a victim of the war, but supported the notion that the true cause of war was foreign powers' envy of the high standard of development in Germany. Various studies have found that in the early years of occupation, many Germans shared the opinion that it was not the Nazis, but the Americans, who "brought real misery to the Germans."[251]

"In the beginning was Goebbels." This is how Bernd Greiner opened his study on the impact and significance of the image of the Morgenthau Plan in the public consciousness. The following legendary quotation from the mouth of the propaganda minister is convincing against the background of an ideologically grounded perception: "Hatred and revenge of a truly biblical nature can be seen in the plans cooked up by the American Jew, Morgenthau. Industrialized Germany is literally to be converted into a huge potato field."[252]

The concept of Germany as a potato field spread like wildfire. Not only did it become popular at all different lev-

els of society, but it even made its way into respectable history books. It didn't even stop at the anti-Western, barbed-
wired entanglements of the former GDR. In a historical
documentation of "policies of the imperialist Western powers toward Germany" from 1952, the familiar image was
borrowed from the Nazi period, though adapted to an anti-imperialist context. It was titled *Die Feinde der deutschen
Nation* (Enemies of the German Nation) and it in, the alleged "Morgenthau Plan" was described as follows: "Not a
trace is supposed to remain of Germany!" and "Satanical
nonsense in the USA . . . Insane destruction hysteria that
was virtually bred during the war in the USA and England.
. . . That is unadulterated, imperialist power politics."[253]

It is true, jarring East German propaganda against
"Anglo-Americans" at the dawning of the cold war might
be just as insignificant in making a fundamental judgment
of Germany's attitude toward America as claimed philo-
and pro-Americanism of the young Federal Republic. But
in any case, there is no question that despite all the later
America-worship in West Germany, traditional anti-American clichés continued to exist and were even intensified
through the war experience.[254] The perceived threat from
the East did surprisingly little to change that. On the contrary, it was incorporated into existing interpretations and
the Americans were given a good share of blame for the
fact that Germany seemed especially threatened in their
conflict with the Soviets.

A 1953 article in the American magazine *Commentary*
clearly illustrated the mood during the early phase of the
cold war: "German Anti-Americanism: East and West
Zones." Back then the West German and East German republics were consolidated into their respective political
blocs. The break that came with the Korean War had already taken place, though debate on integration into the
West was far from completed.

It is striking how the American expert on Germany writing for *Commentary* described West Germany's political restraint toward the West, combined with a type of inner equidistance to the Americans and the Russians. This stemmed from a fear that America's confrontational politics toward the Soviets threatened Germany insofar as the country would be directly involved in war in the case of a military conflict. At the same time the author was overwhelmed with complaints that America does too little in warding off communism.[255]

This ambivalence was joined by traditional reservations—intensified, of course, since they were directed at an occupying power. Americans were viewed the same way as the Russians—albeit as less primitive—not only from the perspective of those defeated in 1945. Both Russians and Americans were regarded as "childish," "naive," and "mentally retarded." From the standpoint of an anti-modern critique of civilization, Moscow and Washington differed at most in the methods they employed in striving to implement their alienating conceptions of civilization. The observer came to the startling conclusion that anti-Americanism was spreading and could be encountered in all social classes and political parties of the early Federal Republic.

This need not necessarily lead to such an assessment. On the other hand, evidence provided by the author was not all that far-fetched, for instance, when he referred to popular literature and traced its popularity back to traditional aspects of anti-Americanism. Among this literature, some of which was written in the United States, he included Stefan Heym's novel *Crusaders* (translated into German as *Der bittere Lorbeer*), in which an American Army captain commits rape and does black market dealing, taking them for granted as a victor's prerogative; a sadistic sergeant also goes about his business, and a hypocritical major appears as an agent of Wall Street. Ernst von Salomon's *Der Fragebogen* (The Questionnaire), written in 1951, was another example of literary anti-Americanism, since the American occupation soldiers were characterized as corrupt, stupid, and brutal.

Other similar literary images of Americans in Germany can be cited. In Wolfgang Koeppen's novel *Tauben im Gras* (Pigeons in the Grass),[256] the character of Ms. Behrend, who runs a grocery store, contemplates about the inferiority of American civilization. It annoys her that "the Amis"* requisition her villa. They lack culture, showing no respect in the way they live in the old German splendor: "Feet up on the tables . . . assemble-line meals . . . the foreign children playing in the yard: bright blue, golden yellow, fire red . . . seven-year-old girls with lips painted like whores, the mothers in overalls . . . itinerant, frivolous people."[257] The outwardly directed nonchalance of the American soldiers is pointedly criticized. "Too much freedom; running wild." The character asks herself, surprised, how these soldiers could ever have won the war, and she comes to the popular conclusion that "it was only on account of the technology and thus a worthless victory. The better soldiers were the Germans."[258]

The *Commentary* author did not only use widespread attitudes—also used in literature—to discuss his concern for the state of the German consciousness; he also wrote about big politics, such as the attitudes of the parties. He wrote that the traditional Social Democratic Party (SPD) in opposition to the ruling Christian Democrats, showed a nationalist, neutral** reserve with respect to America. Even

---

* Amis: pronounced *ah'-meez;* short for "Americans." Similar to "Yankees," frequently pejorative; often used in Germany—trans.
** Nationalist, neutral: A phrase often appearing in the following. In the German *"national-neutral,"* these two aspects are definitely interrelated, referring to a political stance leaning toward neutrality regarding the East-West conflict, from a German-centered, national perspective—trans.

Ernst Reuter, SPD mayor of Berlin, feared that his party would not prove immune to Soviet temptation. In another sense as well, anti-Western reactions became noticeable. Directly following the war, Americans were accused of wanting to introduce capitalism to Germany. Later, there was mention of a "restoration" favored by the occupation forces, as if Germans would have to do without the blessings of socialism from then on. Social Democratic restraint toward America was explained to American visitors as being justified since the ruling parties under Adenauer had sold themselves to the United States and the West to such a degree that differences had to be focussed upon for reasons of opposition alone. With respect to integration with the West, considerable differences between Adenauer's position and that of the Social Democrats could be distinguished. When the social democrat Kurt Schumacher called Konrad Adenauer a "chancellor of the Allies," it was not merely unreflected polemics; it struck a nerve. But to conclude in turn that Adenauer was totally devoted to the political culture of the West would mean overlooking the chancellor's deep occidental, Catholic ties. Adenauer's primary aim was to integrate West Germany institutionally with the political West. With respect to cultural affairs, however, the chancellor maintained an inner reserve, despite an outward willingness to work together with the classical Western democracies. This was clearly demonstrated by his admitting in retrospect that he viewed the West German constitution, the Basic Law, as "very poor." Why? Because it was supposedly imposed upon the West Germans by the Americans and the French.[259]

The observations of the American *Commentary* writer were not limited to the Western part of Germany, but applied as well to East Germany, which he also referred to as the "East Zone." He considered the public there pro-American by the mere fact that a majority of the population opposed the regime. The anti-American stance of the GDR leadership was essentially the same as in other communist regimes in Eastern Europe. Nevertheless, a particular aspect stood out, as already shown through the example of the hysterical Morgenthau attack. The anti-imperialism of East Germany, based on Marxism-Leninism, used images and metaphors that could just as easily have been employed during the Nazi period. For example, in 1948, East German party leader Walter Ulbricht adopted a nationalist tone by accusing the "representatives of U.S. monopoly capital" of intensively working to "divide and dismember Germany. They want a fragmented, powerless Germany on whom they can impose their conditions and their selfish interests."[260]

Speech filled with hostility toward the "Anglo-Americans" was passed down and often used in the early years of the Soviet Occupation Zone/East Germany. In any case, Americans were considered capable of the very worst. When East Germany was also struck by a widespread potato blight in 1950, the Americans were accused of being the well-poisoners, the causes of the plague. A hysterical campaign ensued, charging that U.S. airplanes scattered the potato bugs over East Germany. Supposedly, the procedure was a military maneuver in biological warfare as well as a diabolical campaign to raise profits for the major U.S. chemical companies.[261]

The consequences of the bug infestation throughout East Germany were indeed very extensive. This was primarily due to the fact that large portions of the pesticide stores had been sent to other socialist brother nations that had also been struck by the plague.

It seemed to go without saying that Americans were capable of such a deed—the bombing during the war had obviously made a lasting impression on the collective memory. In view of the potato bug blight it was hardly surprising that Bert Brecht drafted a poem *"Die Amiflieger"* (The Ami flyers):[262]

Sister, come on	Schwester, so komm doch
And leave your dolly be!	Und laß dien Püppchen stehn!
Run, run, look in the sky	Lauf, lauf, am Himmel
There's something nice to see.	Da ist was Schön's zu sehn.
On our backs we want to lie.	Wollen auf dem Rücken liegen
Beyond the field our eyes ascend.	Und sehn hoch übers Feld
The Ami flyers fly on by	Die Amiflieger fliegen
Silver in the firmament.	Silbrig im Himmelszelt.
Mother, I am hungry.	Mutter, ich bin hungrig.
How long until the break?	Wie lang ist's zur Jause hin?
Mother, I don't know	Mutter, ich weiß nicht
Why my stomach aches.	Warum ich so hungrig bin.
The Ami flyers flying	Die Amiflieger fliegen
Silver in the sky	Silbrig im Himmelszelt:
On the fields in Germany	Kartoffelkäfer liegen
Potato bugs do lie.	In deutschem Feld.

Such an intentional merging of past and present was an expression of a peculiar nationalistic reinterpretation of the history of World War II. In the early postwar period, the GDR leadership praised the Soviet Union as the only power that had defeated "fascism." With the intensification of the East-West conflict and the Korean War, a different aspect of that past was called to mind, which upset the composition of the alliance: the criminal nature of "Anglo-Americans," who were stigmatized in the collective consciousness as having reduced German cities to ash and rubble. At the ruins of the Frauenkirche, the Church of Our Lady, in Dresden, a continuity in German history that had otherwise been disputed by the regime, was immortalized:

Church of Our Lady in Dresden
destroyed in February 1945

by Anglo-American bombers
Built by George Bähr
1726—1743
Its ruins commemorate
tens of thousands of lives and urge
the living to fight
imperialistic barbarism
for happiness and peace among humanity.[263]

British and American fire-bombing of German cities during the Second World War continues to serve as an underlying motif in the German collective memory. Although it remained essentially repressed because of its feared association to nationalist and even Nazi attitudes, this image had and still has a subtle—and redirected—impact, especially when attempts are made to chastise Americans for their actions in remote areas of the world, most recently during the 1991 Gulf War. Memories of the bombing of German cities then come back to the surface, along with related sentiments that had remained hidden for decades.

During the Federal Republic period of German history, up to 1989, a specific form of anti-Americanism catches the eye: identification of the United States with German Nazism and its crimes. Such an association is by no means direct or blunt. It can be rather be viewed as a sign of underlying discourse—a pattern for interpreting reality. Not only does this imagined reality portray the United States as the cause of all present-day injustices. According to the logic of rhetorical use of images, metaphors, and relevant formulas, the ultimate—and social—culpability of that which normally falls within the responsibility of the Nazis is thus passed on to the United States.

However, it is a dubious endeavor to ascribe this to the phenomena of political culture in Germany alone, especially since after the Second World War, in general and far beyond Germany's borders, a pattern of behavior developed in which the crimes of the Nazis became a symbol for the worst of all possible things in any situation. And for a long time, many people considered and still consider the United States as the worst of all things. For example, a past Sandinista hymn refer to the United States as the "enemy of humanity" *per se.*

Despite this universal spread of anti-Americanism, a kind of projection can be identified in Germany that exists nowhere else in the same form. The enigmatic identification of the United States with the crimes committed by Nazi Germany represents quite a rarity, even if ideological prejudices often have similar structures: Separating off a negativity and projecting it onto the contrary Other.

The subliminal negative identifications differ in type and frequency; they might be presented in a carefree and naive manner, such as Hermann Hesse's mention in a letter to Thomas Mann in 1946 of his satisfaction that "the criminals and black marketeers, the sadists and the gangsters in Germany are no longer Nazis and they no longer speak German; they are Americans."[264] The images might be literary or have an air of being an innocent, respectable contemporary account, using the genre of a travelogue or a report to give insight into the land of "everyday fascism." And, of course, this phenomenon appears as an anti-imperialistic worldview whenever—such as in the case of Vietnam—America inevitably is accused of committing Nazi crimes.

On top of that, another motif has also been passed down from the parents' generation: the unconscious expectation of being held accountable after the fact for the crimes of the fathers. It is a feeling of awaiting punishment, and the United States is imagined to carry out that punishment. This is confirmed by images and metaphors that were used in protests against American arms race policy in the early 1980s as well as during the 1991 Gulf War. On both occasions, the United States was accused of crimes against humanity, whereas Germany slipped into the role of a historical victim. Especially during the Gulf War, following on the heels of German unification, a type of criticism resembling traditional anti-Americanism could be heard louder than ever before.

Traditional anti-Americanism in Germany was on very unfriendly terms with pre-unification West Germany. In a wide variety of publications, West Germany was portrayed as an American creation. The founding fathers were virtually condemned as traitors. Such an attitude was by no means limited to the extreme right wing. It was just as common within the conservative spectrum as it was in left-leaning circles and among those definitely identifying themselves as left-wing. The following distinct, anti-American positions serve to illustrate this.

The more nationalist, conservative variant can be demonstrated by *"Charakterwäsche. Die amerikanische Besatzung in Deutschland und ihre Folgen"* (Characterwashing: The American occupation in Germany and its consequences), written in 1965 by Caspar Schrenck-Notzing. The author complained that the "reeducation" policies of the Allies were a form of national emasculation.

Another variant is represented by the 1971 polemic by playwright Rolf Hochhuth, *Krieg und Klassenkrieg* (War and Class War). The title alone reveals the specific genre of the work. It combines left-wing and conservative images of America, and precisely by linking issues of the Left and the Right, the real subject comes to light: Hochhuth's book can be used to demonstrate how anti-American images are used in national discourse, independent of political orientation. As a critic of the West German state of affairs who dramatizes historically taboo subjects and social injustice, Rolf Hochhuth is identified with attitudes that are more likely associated with the Left. But Hochhuth is in reality a conservative who suffered more from the division of Germany than from anything else, considering it national humiliation. *Krieg und Klassenkrieg* can be considered anti-imperialistic, but Hochhuth meant the German national question—with anti-American intent.

The most recent of several publications by Rolf Winter dealing with the United States can serve as another example of the impact of traditional anti-Americanism in the pre-unification Federal Republic. His book, published in 1989, is titled *Ami Go Home: Plädoyer für den Abschied von einem gewalttätigen Land* (An appeal to part from a violent land), the meaning of which is perfectly clear. It is an expression of the anti-American mood of the 1980s, spurred on by the debate on the deployment of the American medium range ballistic missiles in Europe. Winter considers himself clearly part of the left and most people would probably agree.

Each of these three works dealt with the relationship between America and Germany and with the United States itself at a different phase of West German development. Despite all differences, they reveal considerable common ground, both in tenor and choice of imagery, for example in the major complaint that the founding of the Federal Republic was in itself an act of treason. The left-identified Winter opened his book with a nationalist thunderbolt: "The Federal Republic is an American product."[265] There were supposedly no Germans among the founding fathers. The Basic Law is a foreign constitution imposed on the [German] people, which "destroyed the nation." And that's not all. Even with respect to the articles of the Basic Law, "permission of the Americans and their allies had to be obtained first."[266] And anyway, everything was orchestrated behind the scenes and against the will of the people by the Americans—not only in 1949, but ongoing. Anyone "wanting political influence in the Federal Republic does

not question 'our American friends, whom we have to
thank for the reconstruction of our fatherland.'"[267] Making
trusty reference to psychoanalyst Horst-Eberhard Richter,
Winter spoke of present-day Germans as "spiritually half
American."[268]

With respect to the founding of the Federal Republic,
Winter's interpretation barely differs from Hochhuth's.
Hochhuth, too, constantly suspected cabal coming from
America and blind subjugation in this country. He saw
Adenauer as a traitor to the nation, the "Rhineland sepa-
ratist." The chancellor supposedly carried out that which
no German should have ever been a party to, according to
the opinion he cited from American columnist Walter
Lippmann. For the sake of national balance, Hochhuth also drew Walter Ulbricht into the charge of high treason.
Both of them, in Hochhuth's opinion, signed oppressive
contracts that chained their respective partial countries to
Washington or Moscow. Just as German princes had once
subjugated themselves to the primacy of religion and
stirred up their subjects to hate one another for true faith,
"these ideologues have betrayed German interests in favor
of enemy foreigners, for whom our country is at best an object to be exploited and at worst a theater of war, where
they can wage battles that are not fought for Germans...."[269]

Hochhuth did not maintain such a national equidistance to both the Americans and the Soviets for very long.
The United States was soon accused of far more terrible
atrocities. The prerequisites "for perpetuating the division
of Germany [have been] deliberately planned by the profi-
teers across the Atlantic...," for which the Soviet threat
provided at most a "plausible justification." From that
point on, according to Hochhuth, the American "governors
of capitalism"[270] pillaged western Germany contemptibly.
By keeping exchange rates high, the Federal Republic was
torn apart outright by the sharks of U. S. capital. "This cur-

rency and labor fraud clearly shows the 'honesty' of the partnership between the giant Uncle Sam and the plain, honest German."[271]

In order to extensively illustrate the humiliating relationship of subjugation, Hochhuth borrowed profusely from Leo L. Matthias, whose American reconnaissance Hochhuth obviously valued highly; in any case he declared his sincere thanks to the doyen and expressed absolute agreement, especially with Matthias's analogy to Latin America.[272]

Whereas Hochhuth did not want to totally ignore the historical context in his attack on America, i.e., "that the Americans came as liberators,"[273] Schrenck-Notzing, who later became the publisher of the right-wing magazine *criticon*, was not tortured by such reservations. Just the opposite is more likely the case, for instance, when he intimated that the postwar plans of the Americans represented something like the "final solution of the German question."[274] He was particularly infuriated by the plans to "reeducate" the Germans. Spitefully, he did not attack the Americans alone, whom he also held responsible for the war; even more, he saw the re-emigrants who had fled to the United States to escape Hitler as powers working to change Germany according to their tastes; and their product was the Federal Republic. He revealed this circle of people to be the initiators of the "characterwashing" that the Germans had to put up with after the war and during the American occupation. This manipulation of German psyches led to the loss of their proven selves. The "character reformers wanted nothing else but to ultimately change the German nature."[275] Schrenck-Notzing included above all the following groups among the so-called character reformers: psychologists, sociologists, and political scientists. The former were supposed to take control of the soul and behavior. The outward, i.e. institutional, adaptation of the Germans to the

West, in Schrenck-Notzing's view, was the responsibility of political scientists, who tried to convey anti-traditional if not utterly reprehensible patterns of thought and values to the subjugated Germans. Setting up professorships for political science and filling the positions with former refugees served as a kind of portal of entry for foreign bodies of thought.[276]

Schrenck-Notzing considered Theodor W. Adorno, et al.'s *Studies in Prejudice* to be a catechism of the American reeducation strategy. On top of everything, Max Horkheimer had been commissioned to do the study in 1944 by the American Jewish Congress.[277] The "eradication of prejudice" in the sense of "reeducation" was optimistically mentioned in the preface. It was of little interest to Schrenck-Notzing that Adorno, et al.'s study on the "authoritarian personality" dealt essentially with anti-Semitism in the United States. The concept of "reeducation" simply appealed to him and the combination of Jewish emigrants in the United States and later use of the term in American occupation politics in Germany was like a godsend for him.

Schrenck-Notzing also made discoveries elsewhere, such as in writings by Kurt Lewin, distinguished social psychologist and Gestalt practitioner. According to Schrenck-Notzing, it was not without reason that Lewin spoke of a "culture change," which would affect all areas of "national life."[278] What he meant by that was not elaborated upon, but the impression remained that the German people were supposed to undergo a downright operation on their consciousness. Schrenck-Notzing felt it was obvious that the "laboratory for the planned character-washing" was constructed in the "Library of Congress in Washington."[279] Using social psychology and political science, the Germans were supposedly subjected to a "second denazification."

The American "retaliatory and reeducation politics"[280] took on a different form in the American-occupied part of Germany. Aside from social psychology and education, the political sciences were supposed to play a major role. "A wonderful example is the 'political science' department, which was recently introduced in all German universities. There were two driving forces behind the new subject area: the Social Democratic government in the state of Hesse and the American military government." In September 1949, the Hessian government organized a conference to discuss the introduction of political science at all German universities, not just those in Hesse. Schrenck-Notzing remarked that the proceedings of the conference sounded ironic. The German professors of the established scholarly tradition that were present requested clarification as to whether political science was truly a science and if it was methodologically structured. The American who was there as an "adviser" interrupted the cautiously developing debate with the remark that political science had to be a true science, alone due to the fact that professorships, institutes, and journals in the field existed in the United States. "Professor Kurt Loewenstein, representative of the military government, added that one shouldn't look a gift horse in the mouth, and the Americans would agree to cover the financing to establish the new science and hire personnel."[281]

And thus it came to be that the new "reeducation science," called "democracy science" by well-meaning people, was forced upon the Germans, and "according to the law that had the departments established, political science continued to develop," wrote Schrenck-Notzing, ironically. First, all available department chairs were filled with former emigrés from America, who did not seem to find it necessary upon returning to Germany to give up either their positions in the United States or their American citizenship. "In southern Germany, the department chairs

were filled in this way in Heidelberg (Carl Joachim
Friedrich), Freiburg (Arnold Bergstraesser), Munich (Eric
Voegelin), and Stuttgart (Golo Mann). Later on, these professors were succeeded by their students (most of whom
studied in the United States)."[282] Schrenck-Notzing seemed
to find the work of Franz Neumann to be especially reprehensible. Neumann was the author of *Behemoth*, one of the
first comprehensive studies on the Nazi regime. Not only
did he work for the American intelligence organization
OSS (Office of Strategic Services) during the war, dealing
with Germany and the process of democratization for the
period after the war, he also actively carried out "reeducation." He was an "American contact at the Free University
in Berlin" and played a substantial role in establishing the
Institute for Political Science there.[283] Schrenck-Notzing
saw such "reeducation" and fostering of the westernization of Germany as "breeding mistrust against power (especially one's own)."

On top of everything, German consciousness was fur-
nished with a corresponding sense of history, devised by
the Americans. They established the Institute for Contemporary History in Munich, and Hans Rothfels, who returned from the United States in 1951, took over the "intellectual command." Rothfels was a person who, in
Schrenck-Notzing's opinion, had the advantage of combining the emigration experience in America with the world
of Prussian nobility, and forming an ideology from the "ar-
tificial synthesis of anti-totalitarianism."[284]

The publication year of Schrenck-Notzing's book is significant: 1965. The student movement had not yet crystal-
lized, though its "spiritual fathers" were suspected later
among the alleged "reeducators" and their critical theories.
It is true that a significant segment of the protest movement that later developed was inspired by those who had
contemplated the democratization process for Germany

during their exile in the United States. The tragedy of the circumstances, perhaps even an unconscious reaction to counter their fears, brought with it the fact that the protest generation that emerged out of the fate of the re-emigrants in turn rebelled against its spiritual fathers, casting their historical experience to the winds. As if in a biographically directed "return," they attacked the United States as the incarnation of everything that traditional hostilities had long since considered typical for America: alienation, capitalism, crime. Lest we forget: the country denounced in this way was the one whose military efforts were substantial in defeating Nazism and the one which contributed to the survival of their teachers.

The critical innocence of those opposing America had two roots. First, it fed upon the theoretical pool made available by the re-emigrants themselves; second, it was reinforced by traditional reactions to America in the collective memory. The ideas of, for example, Horkheimer and Adorno, on theories of culture were used to chastise the "barbarism of the culture industry" in America, while the barbarism in one's own history sank into the shadows of the most general criticism of capitalism.[285]

What could be resolved as a misunderstanding in light of the times in the reception of Horkheimer and Adorno, was confirmed to some extent when the revolutionary metaphors of Herbert Marcuse were adopted literally. The experienced pessimism of the *Dialectic of Enlightenment*, on the other hand, changed the means into an activism that construed America as the universal stronghold of alienation and sought refuge in the Third World. A tragic nonsimultaneity separated the critical theorists from their epigones. Both Horkheimer and Adorno, as was recognized by an astute observer, saw while in America that "history as 'America' had come to an end. But a demythologized America in the European future would take the ec-

static quality out of the revolutionary visions."[286] The fact
that the students were so unresponsive to such insight was
likely due to an event that gave all hostility the appearance
of reason and self-preservation: the Vietnam War.

The war in Vietnam blatantly belied the democratic
and anti-colonial ethos of America. And even more: the actions in Vietnam revived a barely reflected upon memory
of that which, in the language of morality, had become the
epitome of a universal crime—the crimes of the Nazis. This
kind of metaphor was used around the world, though
against the historical background in Germany it lost the
character of random polemics and served as an exonerat-
ing projection. The crimes committed in Vietnam became
interwoven with those of the fathers. Within the context of
a history of guilt viewed as generalizable, the United States
was burdened with precisely that which was difficult to accept in one's own history.

In any case, the subject of guilt was in the air. Hans
Magnus Enzensberger, for one, took up the subject in an
analysis of the times and ended up impacting an entire
generation.

Enzensberger's involvement with America goes back
to the time prior to the Vietnam War. Right in the tradition
of Bert Brecht, he was fascinated by the typically American
blending of "politics and crime"—as a 1964 volume of his
theoretical articles and essays was titled (Politik und Verbrechen). His go-getting interest—going back to the late
1950s—was also directed at the meshing of nuclear destruction and cold, scientific calculation.[287] His observations can essentially be reduced to the threatening poten-
tiality of mass crimes. One essay in the volume mentioned
draws a connection between the incriminating actions of
America and the mass crimes of the Nazis. In "Reflexionen
vor einem Glaskasten" (Reflections Before a Glass Case),
supposed parallels are drawn between Adolf Eichmann

and Herman Kahn, the American mathematician and nuclear strategist who wrote a book in 1961 on the calculability of survival chances in a thermonuclear war.[288]

The ability to universalize horror was reduced to the concept of fascism, which more and more started eclipsing the word "Nazism." Enzensberger's 1968 essay *"Über die Schwierigkeiten, ein Inländer zu sein"* (On the Difficulty of Being a Native) made his opinion crystal clear: "Fascism is not hideous because the Germans practiced it, but because it is possible everywhere."[289] The horror of Nazism referred to as fascism thus does not lie in its past reality, but in its future possibility. And what country could better become the parade ground for such future visions of horror than the United States, already ritualized as the enemy of the world, on account of its dirty war in Vietnam?

The denunciation resorted to the basics; the evidence of evil was reduced to a triviality. In any case, Stanley Milgram's experiments appeared to suffice in providing universal validation of the boundless generalization of crime as a constant threat. The message was perfectly clear: any and every housewife could be a mass murderer. Hannah Arendt challenged Enzensberger, rejecting such a trivialization of her theory of the "banality of evil" as inappropriate.[290]

The artistic presentations that followed Enzensberger were essentially plagiaristic, such as Heiner Kipphardt's "Bruder Eichmann" (Brother Eichmann). Using an analogy meant literally, Kipphardt depicted the cold lack of principles of a B-52 commander who thought nothing of carrying out the command to drop his bombs on civilian targets.[291] Or the earlier collage by Reinhard Lettau, which caused quite a stir. Both Kipphardt's fragment and Lettau's essay "Täglicher Faschismus" (Everyday Fascism) appeared in Enzensberger's journal *Kursbuch*.[292] In a pseudorealistic fashion, Lettau diagnosed an approaching American fas-

cism. The "American evidence" reinforced a change in consciousness that had long since been initiated: the projection
of Nazism, dehistoricized as fascism, onto America. Such
unreflected transference soon spread over the country as
the following slogan: "USA-SA-SS"! The projection onto
America of images and metaphors of evil that history had
reserved for Nazism marked the dawn of a new dimension
of anti-Americanism, which does not mean the traditional
form was a thing of the past, however. For example, classical European contempt for Americans was even cultivated
in Lettau's description of the California lifestyle. He wrote:
"Idle old fogies, almost bored to death, wearing brightly
colored, tightly fitting clothing and calling themselves 'senior citizens.' Wave-riding, brown-skinned hulks and giant
blondes; monotonous, brutal music: those are the symbols
of California."[293]

Even the image of the United States—borrowed from
the nineteenth-century anti-American tradition—as a
stronghold of capitalism that has reached the imperialistic
stage experienced a remake with emancipatory intent. In
Verhör in Havanna (Interrogation in Havanna), "American
rule" was referred to by Enzensberger as the "Heimat des
Mehrwerts" (Home of Surplus Value).[294] Another contrib-
utor to Enzensberger's *Kursbuch* spoke of former U.S. president Gerald Ford as the man of the "silent surplus value."[295]*

Enzensberger gave up his fellowship at the Center for
Advanced Studies at Wesleyan University in January 1967,
which signaled his move away from the United States to an
entire generation. It initiated a political shift away from the
west and toward the south. Hans Magnus Enzensberger

---

* "Silent surplus value": A pun connoting America's supposed capitalist interests, replacing the German word *Mehrheit* (majority) with the Marxist term
Mehrwert (surplus value)—trans.

stood for this trend. He left America to go temporarily to Cuba. In an open letter to the president of the university, a "key document" of the relationship of contemporary German intellectuals to America (Uwe Johnson), he presented his reasons for this dramatic turn. He chastised the ruling class of America as the enemy of the world, saying it was fighting over a billion people in an undeclared war and it was waging this war with all means in its power, "from annihilating bombing to the most sophisticated techniques of consciousness manipulation. Its goal is political, economic, and military world domination."[296]

This first move did not remain unchallenged. In his tetralogy *Jahrestage* (Anniversaries), Uwe Johnson found his own way of rejecting the Manichaeism evoked by Enzensberger, including his charge of fascism directed against the United States.[297] Johnson emphasized that this was not a common form of political dissent; in fact, he thought they might even agree on certain points. He saw Enzensberger's phobic reaction to America more as a phenomenon of deep psychological significance. An entire generation had felt attracted to America in an attempt to dissociate itself from the German past, and now, out of emotional disappointment, it was reacting to a current version of American reality, which then appeared as a "utopian horror vision," diametrically opposed to the generation's American ideal.[298]

Gesine Cresspahl is Johnson's central figure in the four-volume novel. Cresspahl's stay in the United States was used as an acid test of her utopias.

A Jewish real estate broker reassured Cresspahl about the neighborhood she was about to move into: the "shvartzes" will certainly be kept out. She was greatly disturbed at hearing such a racist expression from the mouth of a Jew and fled in desparation to take the next plane back to Germany. At the airport in New York she read in a newspaper that West Germany intended to let the murder and mass extermination committed during the Nazi period come under the statute of limitations. This made her stop and think and she cancelled her trip home. It also made her realize that there is no "moral Switzerland," no neutral place beyond her own history, which she longed for as a result of her German heritage.[299]

This demonstrates the serious dilemma of German consciousness after Auschwitz, which fears that every offense, no matter how trivial, and every regrettable instance of social prejudice will trigger a relapse to great big crimes. Enzensberger took refuge in his "moral Switzerland" of the revolution and the acknowledged good guys, in Cuba.

But the Caribbean island was far from free from all traces of the avoided past. Cuba was not only the innocent island of revolutionary salvation, but on top of that it was also a Hispanic country. Not only did it challenge the capitalist Yankees with a socialist utopia, but it continued the Catholic festivals in the Latin tradition in contrast to the despised Prostestant north. The political icon "Cuba" combined two things: revolutionary anti-imperialism and traditional hostility toward everything Anglo-Saxon. The distinction between remnants of traditional anti-American sentiments and optimistic enthusiasm for the revolution became increasingly blurred.

Enzensberger soon abandoned Cuba's mythos of revolution, an action taken earlier and more radically than many of his followers. In critical self-reflection, he renounced enthusiasm in the Third World as mere escapism. Others remained unshakeably loyal to their anti-Americanism. Such attitudes had considerable longevity, especially because of rationalizations that made them seem insightful. This applied especially to the problem of projecting misunderstood categories of Marxist criticism of political economy—interpreted according to conspiratorial theories—onto real references and the personalization of complex social contexts. The most extreme form of such rationalizations combined the denunciation of America as a detestable global Moloch and its identification with Nazism.

The United States was by no means generally identified directly with the crimes of the Nazis, even if traces of such an identification constantly appear. In this regard, the massacre of Native Americans is a common motif. Rolf Winter represented the popular opinion that American settlers anticipated Hitler, "whose 'providence' was a later equivalent of 'manifest destiny' and its barbaric treatment of the Indians by white Americans."[300] Other attempts to equate the crimes can also be found. The Green Party in Nuremberg staged a war crimes tribunal at the height of the arms' deployment debates to pillory American nuclear strategy.[301] Whether, beyond demonstrating concrete moral indignation, this also represented a reaction by the next generation to the national humiliation from 1945 is not to be decided here.

No matter how such presumptuousness equating Nazism and America was really meant, the examples certainly cannot be dismissed as quirks from the fringes. Their deep impact, irrespective of political camp and ticket, speaks against that. For a certain genre of postwar literature, in fact, equating the Nazi German past with the American present was a leitmotif. In Ernst von Salomon's *Fragebogen* and other works of the early years of the Federal Republic, such as Hans Hellmut Kirst and, to some extent, Wolfgang Koeppen and Heinrich Schirmbeck, the notion of comparison was taken very seriously. Von Salomon wrote a new text to Goethe's ode to America: "Good night, my dear women and children/ We are all poor sinners!/ And in your bedtime prayers/ Save some space on your penitential pew/ For the other cannibals:/ America is not any better!"[302] Insofar, identifying the United States with

Nazism, a practice that experienced a revival during the Vietnam War, and denouncing the United States as the epitome of all evil cannot be seen essentially as reactions to the blind enthusiasm for America of the 1950s and 1960s. Unexpectedly, the Left found itself amidst a conservative tradition that had always denounced the Federal Republic as a republic of the Allies or a vassal of U.S. imperialism, comparing it with Nazism. But it did not stop there: the extreme Left suffered dire consequences for having such a worldview. Everyday bourgeois reality was characterized as a fascist beast and combatted in the end by terrorism.

In the mid-1980s, an interpretation—typical for this variant of anti-Americanism—of the causes of misery in the Third World was published: "Genocide against the social revolution. The U.S.-imperialist Bretton Woods system to carry out the Nazi new order."[303] This was by no means meant metaphorically. The author tried in all seriousness to prove that the Americans had merely taken over global Nazi plans to justify a new system of world domination.

Apart from its grotesque thesis, the pamphlet is interesting for totally different reasons. It showed the best side of sociological theories and imperialism critiques that were dominant in the 1970s, levelling out all differences between the United States today and Nazism back then. Regarding the Nazi period, it reported that a "qualitatively new international division of labor between the German metropolises and their peripheries is supposed to rationalize production in the entire Greater Economic Sphere *(Großraum)*."[304] In reference to the present, the International Monetary Fund was charged with deliberate extermination in its Third World politics. In order to thwart a supposedly inevitable "social revolution, . . . the counter strategies of capital, whether Nazi, Keynesian, or New Deal," resort to any means whatsoever "in order to totally liquidate the social conditions for class struggle in greater metropolitan areas, up to and including physical annihilation."[305] An economic explanation for Nazi extermination politics was thus linked with the claim that Nazism and the United States have significant common ground, i.e., globally expanding capital in the form of imperialism.

Similar theorems inspired by East Germany appeared in between, which found appreciative emulators in West Germany. It was implied in all seriousness that secret service conversations during the final phase of World War II took place between Nazi emissaries in Switzerland and U.S.-American agents in order to pass couriers of the imperialist world enemy on to the Americans. Military perseverence in the final months of the war was supposedly already serving the "imperialist rationality" of the next war.[306] *Autonomie,* a magazine that viewed itself as much more radical, went all out in declaring that the claims of the "anti-Hitler coalition" of World War II had proven to be blatant eyewash. The Americans wanted nothing else than to set up their world domination; the Soviets already showed themselves to be treacherously revisionist.

Henry Morgenthau, Jr. was also the recipient of new dubious honors. Morgenthau, a target of Goebbels's propaganda campaign and general war propaganda, was, according to the magazine, in reality interested "in finding new spheres of influence for the dollar, protected by advancing tanks. He did not neglect to connect the imperial worldview with handsome profits from the very beginning. The mercilessly imposed overvaluation of the dollar relative to the lira after the occupation of Italy is perhaps the most drastic example. Embarrassing English intrigues or reactionary alliances in hopeless rearguard action against the dollar offered the onslaught of the dollar democracy additional ideological ammunition. One after another, Morgenthau duped the exile governments with his ruthless claim to monetary domination."[307]

Such anti-imperialistic revisionism from the left wing in explaining the Second World War taught naive contemporaries better: "We can learn from the obvious linkage of money technology and extermination in New Order Nazi imperialism where it is possible to lift the monetary veil covering the civilized extermination technology of the New Order of Bretton Woods."[308]

The 1970s represented the peak of anti-imperialism that blamed the United States with all conceivable atrocities. This explanation of the world shifted in the 1980s, as economic theories took a serious dive in popularity. The "peace movement" largely refrained from using economic justifications in favor of moralizing ethics. Despite this shift in paradigms, one thing remained the same: America was World Enemy No. 1.

The "peace movement" only superficially introduced new political discourse. Totally in keeping with its pacifist self-image, the movement was globally oriented and thus aimed at worldwide disarmament. Nevertheless, the German-centered perception took on greater significance. It could be argued that the concrete circumstances, that is, the deployment of the new weapons, threatened primarily Germany. But the anti-arms aspect that increasingly perceived Germany to be in a special situation was not all that new either. Arguments of the contemporary peace movement included trends that had already been virulent in the 1950s. Showing latent neutralism, the movement sought a way out of the confrontation of the political blocs, which were considered aggressively opposed to peace. In addition, nationalist currents could be made out below the surface, even if movement supporters would never say that was intended. Against the background of free-floating hostilities, the very reason for the protest steered activity in that direction, like it or not. This was brought to light by the merging of traditionally left-wing and right-wing arguments.[309]

In the 1950s the rumor already persisted that the two superpowers, especially the United States, intended to turn Germany into a battlefield of their rivalry. Not that a conceivable military confrontation between the two blocs would have spared Germany. After all, Germany had the greatest density of lethal materials stored there. In view of the political, geographical, and strategic circumstances of the East-West conflict, such a remark seems trivial; the drawing of a line through Europe that separated the blocs was not least because of Germany. But the anti-American sentiments that predominated in the peace movement implied even more. For example, the assumption—which certainly might be worthy of discussion—that Washington was considering a strategic break from a now-vulnerable Europe by deploying the new missiles. There were also more wild ideas according to which America was even willing to accept the destruction of Germany in order to secure its threatened world domination. And the notions went even further. More and more, anti-nuclear discourse started including other areas such as the German national issue. The rumor went around that Germany was an occupied nation, and the people who spread the rumor were not anonymous.

Honorable personalities helped to develop such attitudes, such as theologist Helmut Gollwitzer, minister and former mayor of Berlin Heinrich Albertz, and theologist Dorothe Sölle. Such ecclesiastic support distinguished themselves through both their pacifism and their patriotism. Other groups, including some that were actually more qualified on the issue, soon distinguished themselves among those who had become active regarding the national issue. Rudolf Augstein, publisher of Germany's famous liberal magazine *Der Spiegel*, who always had nationalist, neutral leanings saw the Federal Republic in nuclear

hostage, a preferred "site for maneuvers and battle . . .
glacis for the French and the Americans." Like waking up
after a deep doze, Germany was once again spoken of as a
protectorate, an American colony, even a "military colony."
Gollwitzer had the presumption to suggest that deploying
the missiles represented unconditional subjugation to foreign interests, "handing over authority for the existence of
our people to a foreign government." No German could accept that. Minister Albertz viewed the failure to demonstrate total sovereignty and the lack of a peace treaty as the
real reasons for Germany to be subjugated to the will of the
superpowers. Sölle, on the other hand, took up the nationalist, neutral jargon of the 1950s by complaining that all the
problems came from the fact that Adenauer "sold us out as
it were to the Americans." There was disparaging talk of
the "governors in Bonn," who were obedient to the American warmongers. Sölle used the oldest of anti-American
phrases, which had not sold for ages, as if suffering from
historical repetition compulsion. She demagogically spoke
of evil having "an address and a telephone number. Evil is
not anonymous and is not at work just anywhere. It can be
named. We know who destroyed Hiroshima, not to mention Nagasaki. We can find out which senators in the
American Senate support the arms race and are profiting
from it." The Manichaean interpretation was expanded to
include the entire Western alliance. Alfred Mechtersheimer, a nationalist, conservative member of the Green
Party bluntly declared that NATO and peace are "fundamentally mutually exclusive."[310] Rolf Winter agreed: America is "a country habitually incapable of peace, constantly
on a crusade." And pro-American attitudes had taken on
an air of treason. When West German politicians spoke of
sharing a system of values with the Americans, it was
nothing but dedicated "satellite argot" according to Winter.[311]

After Gorbachev introduced his politics of glasnost and perestroika, and East and West jointly resolved to dismantle their nuclear arsenals, it could be clearly heard from the ranks of the "peace movement" that in the end it was *their* efforts that led to disarmament. Such a presumption could have been left uncontested if a new injustice had not been waiting after a phase of inner and outward peaceableness, i.e., the 1991 Gulf War.

Despite all similarities between the movements protesting the arms race, on the one hand, and the Gulf War, on the other, there is a significant difference. Whereas the peace movement of the 1980s still had the trusted coordinates of the East-West conflict as a frame of reference, protest against the Gulf War threatened to fall into the pit of its own history. In any case the past appeared to a much greater extent than before. The psychological dangers were obvious: the mood was aimed against America alone, totally and head-on.

Critics of the peace movement were probably right when they did not buy the claimed equidistance to both the United States and the Soviet Union. Actually, America was the lone target of the protest. This essentiality was given free rein during the Gulf War. Whereas the charge of anti-Americanism during the 1980s peace movement had been met with rejecting indignation, no such denial seemed necessary anymore. Alfred Mechtersheimer, former combat pilot in the Bundeswehr, the German army, peace researcher, and politician for the Greens mentioned above, no longer wanted to beat around the bush regarding his aversion to America. In his article *"Antiamerikanisch—weshalb eigentlich nicht?"* (Anti-American? Why on earth not?), he revealed an entire worldview.[312] The contents of Mechtersheimer's divulgence might not necessarily be the most representative of everything that could be heard and read in Germany relating to the Gulf War, but it is significant as an example of lumping together all the elements of historically traditional anti-Americanism. This could also have been documented elsewhere, albeit in a less concentrated and generally more artistic form.

Mechtersheimer was impelled by a familiar anti-American theme: the supposed contrast between self-interest and morality. Within the context of the cold war and the bipolar bloc division, this element took a back burner to the central matter of the nuclear arms race and showing opposition to it. With the end of the East-West conflict, the contrast between justice and power—or rather, between international law and the use of force—starting moving to the foreground more and more. Mechtersheimer's words were chosen specifically with the United States in mind: "What politics thought was justice and freedom, turned out to be unscrupulous power politics, costing death and misery for millions."[313] He made the charge more clear by polemicizing against the institution holding the legal responsibility to authorize internationally warranted use of force: the United Nations. The outcome was obvious: The United Nations does not bring about justice, "but merely legitimizes the notion of might makes right."[314]

The pattern of ethical attitudes prescribing a strict dichotomy of justice and might, morality and self-interest is among the extremely significant themes of anti-Western political culture. The notion of speaking of God and meaning calico was already a common expression in the nineteenth century. No matter what form the thrust assumed, it was always directed against a concept of international law allegedly dominated by Anglo-Saxon tradition. At first it was anti-Wilsonian and opposed to the League of Nations, the principles and institutions of which were received by nationalists throughout the world and the communist Left with biting ridicule at best, though more often deep hatred. In any case, the Nazis were quick to turn their backs on the

League of Nations. The reasons for the step had stayed the same over the ages: international law serves the powerful, the West, the Anglo-Saxons—it serves America.

The United Nations was not spared such animosity. In contrast to the early League of Nations, it did not dissociate itself from Germany and Bolshevist Russia, but included the Soviet Union from the very beginning. In addition, however, the United Nations arose out of a military alliance that was primarily directed against Nazi Germany. The "enemy state clause" in the United Nations Charter is evidence of this specific origin, and, by the way, the history-conscious Mechtersheimer knew to make reference to it. In a passionately democratic display, he presented his objections to the fact that "the four victorious powers from 1945 have veto power," and—together with China—have more power than all the other member countries combined. True to the tradition of anti-Western or anti-American hostility, he recognized common interests between the former Axis powers and the peoples overseas living in the shackles of Western colonialist oppression, for whom the meanwhile obsolete term "Third World" became commonplace in the language of the postwar period. Mechtersheimer attacked the United Nations Security Council as "a power oligarchy to secure antiquated privileges." "It is a cartel against both the economically strengthened war-time enemies of 1945 and the former colonies." Talk of a new world order, he implied, meant nothing more than the reinforcement of the old, albeit modified, postwar order, now beyond the East-West conflict.[315] This merely prolonged the supremacy of the victors in World War II. Their domination threatened to persist beyond the period as a consequence of treason committed by the responsible German politicians. Americanism, the "successful Americanization of the entire world," had also become a "German ailment," according to Mechtersheimer; America was less to blame

than "those on all continents who have not fought against
it, such as the Germans, who developed no resistance since
they lacked their own political identity."[316] By resistance, he
of course meant resistance to the United States, not to the
Nazis.

Emotions were especially heated up in the winter of
1991 by the concept of a "New World Order," coined by
George Bush. Why it came to such outbursts cannot be determined exactly. Actually, he only spoke of the old order
of bipolarity having become obsolete, a reference that must
seem trivial to anyone not blindly tied to the old coordinates of thought and the related perception of reality. Accordingly, Bush's envisaged "New World Order" could only mean that international institutions—especially the
United Nations—would now take on far more weight; relationships between countries would be regulated more
strongly than previously by international law; borders are
to be respected, and, on account of the total decline of ideological opposites, universal recognition of common principles of real political conduct and action is to be strengthened. It is one thing that all of this sounds good in theory;
it is quite different whether this can be easily implemented
in a world of rivalling nation states marked by the spread
of seemingly atavistic ethnic conflicts.

No matter how the phrase "New World Order" might
have been intended, it was met with spiteful reactions
playing on the same old hostility toward the "typical Anglo-Saxon" contradiction between justice and might, self-
interest and morality. The contrast between German and
Anglo-Saxon political mentalities, assumed to be long
since overcome, flared up again. Just as when former president Bush, by mentioning the "New World Order," took
up the linguistic tradition found in Wilson's Fourteen
Points and FDR's Atlantic Charter, segments of the German public reacted idiosyncratically—as if the traditional

contrast of opposites had been confirmed.

Criticism of the "New World Order" did not conclude with the end of the Gulf War. It became tied with the familiar pattern of denunciation whereby, for example, the United States was accused of not intervening in the Balkans solely because there is no oil there. The deep satisfaction of charging America with cold utilitarianism and materialism rather than analyzing the real differences between the conflicts is characteristic of a certain species of ethics, which likes to raise itself above the dirty world into a moral heaven. In contrast to this, Anglo-Saxon and American pragmatism—i.e., constant efforts to balance action-guiding principles and practical demands—apparently must appear to be base treason, and attacking its supposed unscrupulousness was always a central aspect of anti-Western hostility in Germany. In such an apparently theological Manichaeism of morality and anti-morality, pragmatism is in a very bad position.

In view of the Gulf War, many people felt it was clear that the Americans intervened exclusively out of a greedy interest in oil. They zealously adopted a slogan that appeared to have come from the "other America," that is, the protest movement in the United States: "No blood for oil." What happened next was inevitable, following as a matter of course on the heels of transcultural transference of political metaphors: in the changed context, the meaning of the images also changed. Whereas "No blood for oil" might have originally meant that the United States should not risk the lives of American soldiers for real or alleged oil interests, in Germany the slogan existed within a very dubious historical context.

Anton Zischka, a popular non-fiction author in Nazi Germany as well as the postwar period, borrowed the phrase "blood for oil" from Clemenceau to use in his 1939 book *Ölkrieg* (Oil War). The main point of Zischka's popu-

larly written political history of oil exploitation was to reveal the imperialist machinations of England, scoldingly
referred to as "perfidious Albion."[317] Zischka's theory was
as simple as it appeared to be insightful: The greed of the
West—especially England—for oil ultimately led to war.
Germany, on the other hand, supposedly sought synthetic
substitutes for natural resources, not only to minimize its
dependence on foreign sources of raw materials, but in order to counter the exploitation of nature per se. The slogan
"blood for oil" was given an anti-colonial connotation and
used by Zischka in connection with the French policy of
"impoundment"—that is, the occupation of the Ruhr region in 1923, when France strove to use force to secure coal
and wood as reparations payments—thus providing an additional thrust to the development of an anti-Western consciousness in Germany. According to Zischka, the French
pushed through a compensation enterprise at Germany's
expense. That is, they were eager to substitute oil deposits
in northern Iraq with coal from the Ruhr region. The battle
of the Ruhr—a battle for oil in the Middle East shifted to
Germany.[318]

Repetition of the past in exceptional situations, such as
the Gulf War, might suggest that traditional political metaphors represent a significant part of the collective memory,
which surfaces in times of crisis only to later sink back into amnesic depths. It must be taken into account, however,
that an exceptional situation might be a mere coincidence,
even if this is relativized by the historical awareness of the
power of subliminal images.

Peace cannot come from the United States—in any
case, Mechtersheimer was firmly convinced of this. In his
opinion, the United States did not merely have imperialistic politics, it was the epitome of imperialism. And the global Moloch has left a long trail of blood. There is no doubt
about it: "The continuity of U.S. American bloody expan-

sion extends from the extermination of the Native American Indians to the perpetual intervention in Latin America, the war crimes in Dresden and Hiroshima, to Vietnam, all the way to the massacre of Mutla Ridge in February 1991, south of the Iraqi city of Basra." In fact, the "path the United States is taking to world domination" is lined with "hecatombs of victims in the Third World."[319] Actually, the Americans had not waged a correct and thus honorable war against Iraq. Instead, with its superior war machine—size and materials—it was a sheer massacre, according to the cited psychoanalyst Horst-Eberhard Richter. This accusation of America's waging a particularly cruel war gives the impression that he, a declared pacifist, would support a war fought in a somehow "respectable," fair, and noble manner.

Such presumption brings yet another motif of traditional anti-Americanism back to life: the notion that keeps going around of the military incompetence of American soldiers—supposedly balanced out solely by state-of-the-art technology and absolutely inexhaustible reserves of human and material resources. As has already been discussed, this comes from a pronounced reactionary form of anti-Americanism. There are many explanations for it, a central aspect always being a devaluation and trivialization of everything civilian, bourgeois, and commercial. Americans downright lose their nerve.

That sort of perception is anything but peaceable. Seen in the proper light, it belongs among interpretations within a particularly militaristic tradition, of course with the difference that is has now been turned around. This is not a matter of civilians arming themselves in exceptional circumstances, but of deeply engraved militarism, the potential extent of which is to be offset by constant counterphobic rituals of demonstrative peaceableness. No wonder German pacifist self-stylization is met with deep skepticism by Germany's allies—it is based on self-deception. The denied willingness to use force, as a result of the historical trauma, is projected precisely onto the one that has always been seen as the Other and used as a screen on which to project that very denial: the United States.

Rolf Winter, for example, showed his true colors in this regard in the subtitle to his book: "An appeal to part from a violent country." In the book, he compiled a wealth of materials to document the exclusively violent nature of U.S. society—facts which are not being contested here individually. But the book was not written solely to make reference to them. If Winter were driven by concern for the well-being of Americans, which is being worn away by social violence, he would not have named his book *Ami go home*. According to Winter, all violence stems from America.

Anti-Americanism typically displays a peculiar ambivalence. On the one hand, the American superpower is commonly referred to apocalyptically as Global Danger Zone No. 1; on the other hand, the United States is trivialized with regard to the military with an arrogant gesture of superiority. Winter saw it quite that way. Still referring to the time of the East-West conflict, he considered it a given that Americans were not in a position to defend West Germany. In his opinion, the eastern troops were far superior. Wherever U. S. soldiers had been brought into action, they proved to be incompetent. Incompetent in Korea; incompetent in Indochina; incompetent in Beirut and incompetent in Grenada. Even during the Iran-Iraq War in the 1980s, when the "United States once again played world policeman, wanting to guarantee free and safe conduct for the oil tankers, it again turned out to be a demonstration of baffling incompetence."[320]

Winter found the American war industry to be even more incompetent. It obviously produced nothing but junk. Aircraft motors were unreliable, armor-plating for ships was rusty. In the Vietnam War, for example, unnerved American soldiers were "often" forced to arm themselves with Soviet booty after their own automatic hand weapons failed.[321] The Americans were also much indebted to German ingenuity because of their technological incompetence. The author offered the following anecdote as evidence: When the United States ordered one of its new super bombers to the international aircraft fair in Paris, the engines could not be activated for the return flight. "Not until a special device was flown in from Germany could it be started and flown back to Texas."[322] Leo L. Matthias appears to still be right: Aside from the Jeep, the Americans did not contribute much of significance in the area of military technology.

It is no surprise when people reverse such arrogance through pacifist excitement to counter their own fears, such as happened during the 1991 Gulf War. The *Kursbuch*, now open to all political orientations, allowed a voice to those who attempted to portray American military incompetence, in a knowledgeable, ironic fashion—and of course with pacifist intent. As if guided magically by an invisible hand, *Kursbuch* author Asmus Petersen resorted to German soldier talk thought to be long since forgotten, which contrasted the supposed military incompetence of the Americans with the military virtues of the Germans in World War II.

No other military conflict of recent decades did more to revive pictures of the Second World War and the corresponding identifications and counter-identifications than the war at the Persian Gulf. The situation at the Gulf was just as much a *déjà vu* of the world war for the "Allies" as for the indignant pacifist contingent in Germany, which acted out repetition fantasies en masse.

Although written in a pacifist tone, the *Kursbuch* author made no secret of such an analogy. He also did not refrain from taking sides regarding the battlefields of World War

II, at least with respect to military qualifications. In the
tenor of past popular opinion, he wrote: "The 'Amis' have
not learned a thing since 1945." Even then they had to call
for "major artillery support" at the slightest resistance. Asmus Petersen treated the later Lord Montgomery of El
Alamein with the same disrespect: materials instead of
bravery—presumably a despicable Anglo-Saxon affliction.
In any case, according to the author, all of this was repeat-
ed at the Persian Gulf. The "whole thing" just lacked "form
and quality." Schwartzkopf supposedly simply "played it
safe; not a trace of surprise tactics." Petersen alluded to
someone else who once fought in the desert—certainly
"with a lot more imagination and a lot less materials."[323]

Despite all his effort to be ironic, Petersen was not able
to hide the underlying drive of his very traditional anti-
Americanism. In that respect he indeed displayed integri-
ty, albeit against his will. Unfeigned and lacking any irony,
he told of his nightmares triggered by the Gulf War—
dreams in which the area bombing of 1944/45 came back
and the feeling "that goes with it that seemed to have been
forgotten; that low, rhythmic droning of five hundred four-
engine planes approaching at the same time is back
again—although we didn't lose our composure back then
while the cities were being reduced to ashes. Very
strange."[324] Was it really strange?

Anti-Americanism in Germany—and elsewhere—is
fed by many sources. They might have traditional origins,
going far back into the nineteenth century, sometimes even
the eighteenth, and be simply anti-modern. They might be
politically and nationally charged on account of experiences in the First and Second World Wars or rationalized as
a social critique from the left through partisanship in the
Cold War. Hostilities toward America can almost always
be empirically documented—after all, only in isolated cases does it pay to openly admit anti-Americanism. As a

worldview, it was and still is frowned upon.

Whatever—in view of the complex world we live in, the confused consciousness needs America as an omnipotent power, a bastion of intrigue and evil. Such Manichaeism without a doubt makes it easier to find orientation. And anti-Americanism is thus certainly an ideological reduction of complexity.

References have often been made to the earlier critical works of Max Horkheimer, written *before* the horror of fulfilled Nazism, in order for people to better ignore his later and deeply pessimistic ideas. In 1968, at the peak of identity-seeking protest against the Vietnam War, he clearly distinguished between legitimate and historically conscious criticism, on the one hand, and blind anti-Americanism, on the other. He set himself against the attitude taken by many who otherwise professed to sympathize with his ideas. Expanding America to mean the West per se, Horkheimer wrote: "To measure the so-called free world by its own concept, to be critical of it, and nevertheless to support its ideas, to defend it against fascism of the Hitler, Stalin, or any other variety, is the right and obligation of all thinking people. Despite the fateful potential, despite all the injustices within and without, it is still an island, geographically and chronologically, the end of which, in the ocean of tyrannies, would mean the end of the culture of critical theory."[325]

Horkheimer's reference to fascism and Stalinism seems to be somewhat outdated today. But in view of the historical difference between Europe and America, the conclusions that might have been obsolete back then can retain their validity, especially in light of a Europe going through a restoration process in which the furies of nationalism and ethnocentrism once again have room to rage. What was rejected as simply reactionary in 1968, is now valid more than ever.

Notes

Notes for Pages 1-27

1 John Locke, *Two Treatises of Civil Government*, (New York : Cambridge University Press :1966 [1690], II, chap. V, sec. 49).

2 Francisco López de Gómara, *Primera Parte de la Historia General de las Indias*, (Biblioteca de Autores Españoles, vol. 22, Madrid 1852, p. 156; cited in: John Huxtable Elliott, *The Old World and the New, 1492-1650* (Cambridge: Cambridge Universiry Press, 1970), p. 10.

3 Adam Smith, *An Inquiry into the Nature and Causes of the Wealth of Nations*, R. H. Campbell, A. S. Skinner, and W. B. Todd, eds., Glasgow Edition [1776], vol. 2, IV, chap. vii, part c, sect 50 (Oxford: Claridon Press,1976), p. 626.

4 See Durant Echeverria, *Mirage in the West: A History of the French Image of American Society to 1815* (Princeton: Princeton University Press, 1951), p. 116.

5 "Recherches Philosophiques sur les Americains," in *Oevres Philosophiques*, Paris 1974, vol. 1, p. II [1768].

6 Antonello Gerbi, *The Dispute of the New World: The History of a Polemic, 1750-1900* (Pittsburgh: Pittsburgh University Press , 1973) [Milan 1955].

7 John H. Elliott, *The Old World and the New*, p. 5.

8 See a recent summary of European images of America in: C. Vann Woodward, *The Old World's New World*, (New York: Oxford University Press, 1991), p. 4.

9 *Decades*, trans. Richard Eden (1555) in *The First Three English Books on America*, ed. Edward Arber, Birmingham 1885, p. 71; cited in: John H. Elliott, *The Old World and the New*, p. 26.

10 Ludwig Marcuse, "Der europäische Anti-Amerikanismus," in: *Neue Schweizer Rundschau* 21 (1953), pp. 67-73, here: p. 73.

11 Ibid., p. 68.

12 Ignazio Silone, *Fontamara*, London 1985, p. 35, cited in: C. Vann Woodward, *The Old World's New World*, p. 83.

13 Wolfgang Wagner, "Das Amerikabild der Europäer," in: Karl Kaiser, Hans-Peter Schwarz, eds., *Amerika und Westeuropa. Gegenwarts- und Zukunftsprobleme*, (Stuttgart: Belser 1977), pp. 17-28, here: 18. (English translation, Boston: Lexington Books, 1978)

14 Henry Steele Commager, Enrico Giordanelli, *Was America a Mistake? An Eighteenth Century Controversy*, (New York: Harper & Row, 1967), p. 59.

NOTES FOR PAGES 1-27 (CONTINUED)

15 Cited in: Antonello Gerbi, *The Dispute of the New World*, p. 53.
16 C. Vann Woodward, *The Old World's New World*, p. 9.
17 Manfred Henningsen, *Der Fall Amerika. Zur Sozial- und Bewusstseins-geschichte einer Verdrängung,,* (Munich: List 1974), p. 169.
18 Alexis de Tocqueville, *Democracy in America*, 2 vols., (New York: Schocken, 1972 [Paris 1840], vol. 1, p. 265).
19 George W. Pierson, *Tocqueville and Beaumont in America*, New York 1938, p. 748; cited in: C. Vann Woodward, *The Old World's New World*, p. 82.
20 Georg Wilhelm Friedrich Hegel, *The Philosophy of History*, trans. J. Sibree (Introduction trans. by Carl J. Friedrich), (New York: Willey, 1900), pp. 86-87 (Introduction).
21 Manfred Henningsen, *Der Fall Amerika*, (Munich: List, 1974), p. 84.
22 Ernst Fraenkel, *Amerika im Spiegel des deutschen politischen Denkens. Äusserungen deutscher Staatsmänner und Staatsdenker über Staat und Gesellschaft in den Vereinigten Staaten von Amerika*, (Cologne, Opladen: Westdeutscher Verlag, 1959) , p. 24. (a collection of texts, with an introduction). Frank Trommler, "The Rise and Fall of Americanism in Germany", in: Frank Trommler and Joseph Mc-Veigh, America and the Germans. An Assessment of a Three-Hundred-Year History (Philadelphia: University of Pennsylvania Press, 1985) , Vol.II, pp. 332-342.
23 Hannah Arendt, On Revolution (New York: Viking, 1963) pp. 45 ff.
24 Leo L. Matthias, *Die Entdeckung Amerikas oder das geordnete Chaos*, (Hamburg : Rowohlt, 1953).
25 Leo L. Matthias, *Die Kehrseite der USA*, (Reinbek : Rowohlt, 1964).
26 Leo L. Matthias, *Die Entdeckung Amerikas*, p. 10.
27 Ibid., pp. 39, 45.
28 Ibid., p. 47.
29 Ibid., p. 106.
30 Ibid., p. 110, 125.
31 Ibid., p. 134.
32 Ibid., p. 133.
33 Ibid., p. 155.
34 Leo L. Matthias, *Die Kehrseite der USA*, p. 338.
35 Leo L. Matthias, *Die Entdeckung Amerikas*, p. 196.
36 Ibid., p. 249.
37 Ibid., p. 231.
38 Ibid., p. 237.
39 Ibid., p. 231.
40 Ibid., p. 236.
41 Ibid., p. 230.
42 Ibid., p. 162.
43 Ibid., p. 163.
44 Ibid., p. 163.

NOTES FOR PAGES 1-27 (CONTINUED)

45 Ibid., p. 164.

46 Ibid., p. 321.

47 Ibid., pp. 264-66.

48 Ibid., p. 276.

49 Ulrich Ott, *Amerika ist anders. Studien zum Amerika-Bild in deutschen Reiseberichten des 20. Jahrhunderts*, (Frankfurt/Main: Peter Lang, 1991), p. 229.

50 Otto Ladendorf, ed., *Historisches Schlagwörterbuch*, (Strasbourg and Berlin: Tübner, 1906), p. 5. I would like to thank Iring Fetscher for this reference.

51 Max Horkheimer, *Gesammelte Schriften*, vol. 14, (Frankfurt/Main: Suhrkamp,1988), p. 408.

52 Cited in: Paul Hollander, *Anti-Americanism. Critiques at Home and Abroad 1965-1990*, (New York: Oxford University Press,1992), p. 334.

53 Jean Baudrillard, *America*, (New York :Verso, 1988), p. 55.

54 Cited in: Wolfgang Wagner, "Das Amerikabild der Europäer," p. 20.

55 C. Vann Woodward, *The Old World's New World*, p. 81.

56 Ernest Jones, *Free Associations: Memories of a Psycho-Analyst*, 1959, p. 191; cited in: Peter Gay, *Freud: A Life for Our Time*, (New York: W.W. Norton, 1988), p. 563. Frank Trommler, "Freud's America" in: Frank Trommler and Joseph McVeigh, America and the Germans. op. cit,. pp.303-316.

57 Ludwig Marcuse, "Der europäische Anti-Amerikanismus," p. 70.

58 Manfred Henningsen, *Der Fall Amerika*, p. 128.

59 Ernst Fraenkel, *Amerika im Spiegel des deutschen politischen Denkens*, pp. 15-16.

60 Gerhard Weinberg, "Deutschland und Amerika 1917 bis 1949," in: Klaus Weigelt, ed., *Das Deutschland- und Amerikabild*, (Melle: Knoth, 1986), pp. 20-28, here: p. 21.

61 Gerhard Weinberg, "Deutschland und Amerika 1917 bis 1949," p. 24.

62 Michael Jeismann, *Das Vaterland der Feinde. Studien zum nationalen Feindbegriff und Selbstverständnis in Deutschland und Frankreich 1792-1918*, (Stuttgart: Klett-Cotta, 1992), p. 29.

63 Gesine Schwan, "Das deutsche Amerikabild seit der Weimarer Republik," in: *Aus Politik und Zeitgeschichte* 28 (1986), pp. 3-15, here: p. 4.

Notes for Pages 29-51

64 Rolf Engelsing, "Deutschland und die Vereinigten Staaten im 19. Jahrhundert. Eine Periodisierung," in: *Die Welt als Geschichte* 2/3 (1958), pp. 138-156, here: p. 143.

65 Hildegard Meyer, *Nord-Amerika im Urteil des deutschen Schrifttums bis zur Mitte des 19. Jahrhunderts*, (Hamburg : Friedrichsen, de Gruyter, 1929), p. 20.

66 Cited in: Günter Moltmann, "Deutscher Antiamerikanismus heute und früher," in: Otmar Franz, ed., *Vom Sinn der Geschichte*, (Stuttgart:

NOTES FOR PAGES 29-51 (CONTINUED)

Seewald, 1976), pp. 85-105, here: p. 92.

67 Cited in: Hildegard Meyer, *Amerika im Urteil des deutschen Schrifttums*, p. 13.

68 Alfred Kerr, *Yankeeland—Eine Reise,* (Berlin: R. Moss 1925), pp. 89f.

69 Cf. in detail, Manfred Durzak, *Der deutsche Roman der Gegenwart*, (Stuttgart: Kohlhammer, 1973), pp. 319ff.

70 Ulrich Ott, *Amerika ist anders*, p. 85.

71 Nikolaus Lenau, *Sämtliche Werke und Briefe in zwei Bänden,* (Frankfurt/Main: Insel, 1971), vol. 2, p. 207.

72 Ibid., p. 215.

73 Ibid., p. 215.

74 Ibid., p. 216.

75 Ibid., p. 213.

76 Ibid., p. 210.

77 Ibid., p. 207.

78 Ibid., p. 207.

79 Ibid., p. 218.

80 Manfred Durzak, "Nach Amerika Gerstäckers Widerlegung der Lenau-Legende," in: ——, *Das Amerika-Bild der deutschen Gegenwartsliteratur,* (Stuttgart: Kohlhammer, 1979), pp. 38-58, here: pp. 39-40.

81 Cited in: Günter Moltmann, "Deutscher Antiamerikanismus heute und früher," p. 94.

82 Johannes Urzidil, "Das Freiheitsideal," in: Alexander Ritter, ed., *Deutschlands literarisches Amerikabild. Neuere Forschungen zur Amerikarezeption der deutschen Literatur,* (Hildesheim: Olms 1977), pp. 154-203, here: 169-70.

83 *The Complete Poems of Heinrich Heine: A Modern English Version*, trans. Hal Draper, (Boston: Suhrkamp, 1982), p. 633.

84 *The Romantic School and Other Essays*, Jost Hermand and Robert C. Holub, eds., [The German Library, vol. 33] (New York : Continuum, 1985), p. 263.

85 Ibid.

86 Ibid.

87 IIbid., p. 264.

88 On Marx's proximity to Heine, see, for example, Jean Pierre Lefebvre, "Marx und Heine," in: ——, *Heinrich Heine. Streitbarer Humanist und volksverbundener Dichter,* (Weimar:Aufbau 1973), pp. 41-61. More recent, and with an obvious emphasis: Renate Schlesier, "Homeric Laughter by the Rivers of Babylon: Heinrich Heine and Karl Marx," in: Mark H. Gelber, ed., *The Jewish Reception of Heinrich Heine*, Conditio Judaica 1, (Tübingen: Mohr, 1992), pp. 21-43. The following basic study is very instructive: Klaus Briegleb, *Opfer Heine? Versuche über Schriftzüge der Revolution,* (Frankfurt/Main: Suhrkamp, 1986), pp. 71-104.

89 Jost Hermand, "Auf andere Art so grosse Hoffnung. Heine und die

NOTES FOR PAGES 29-51 (CONTINUED)

USA," in: Sigrid Bauschinger, Horst Denkler, Wilfried Malsch, *Amerika in der deutschen Literatur*, (Stuttgart: Reclam, 1975), pp. 81-92.

90   Ibid., p. 52. Cf. also: Gerhard Weiss, "Heines Amerikabild," in: Alexander Ritter, ed., *Deutschlands literarisches Amerikabild. Neuere Forschungen zur Amerikarezeption der deutschen Literature*, (Hildesheim: Olms,1977), pp. 295-318, here: p. 308.

91   Heinrich Heine, *Sämtliche Schriften*, vol. 3 (Munich: Hanser, 1971), p. 122.

92   Heinrich Heine, *Sämtliche Schriften*, vol. 2 (1969), p. 72.

93   Ibid., p. 380.

94   Jost Hermand, "Auf andere Art so grosse Hoffnung," p. 85.

95   Heinrich Heine, *Sämtliche Schriften*, vol. 3 (1971), pp. 116-117.

96   Heinrich Heine, *Historisch-kritische Gesamtausgabe der Werke*, Manfred Windfuhr, ed., vol. 11: "Ludwig Börne. Eine Denkschrift," Helmut Koopmann, ed. (Hamburg : Hoffmann & Campe,1978), pp. 35ff.

97   Gerhard Weiss, "Heines Amerikabild," p. 314.

98   See also Manfred Durzak, "Traumbild und Trugbild Amerika. Zur literarischen Geschichte einer Utopie. Am Beispiel von Willkomms 'Europamüden' und Kürnbergers 'Amerika-Müde,'" in: ———, *Das Amerika-Bild in der deutschen Gegenwartsliteratur*, pp. 16-37.

99   Rüdiger Steinlein, "Ferdinand Kürnbergers 'Der Amerika-Müde.' Ein 'amerikanisches Kulturbild' als Entwurf einer negativen Utopie," in: Sigrid Bauschinger, et al., *Amerika in der deutschen Literatur*, pp. 154-177, here: p. 155.

100 See also Frank Trommler, "Vom Vormärz zum Bürgerkrieg. Die Achtundvierziger und ihre Lyrik," in: Sigrid Bauschinger, et al., *Amerika in der deutschen Literatur*, pp. 93-107.

101 Ferdinand Kürnberger, *Der Amerikamüde*, Friedemann Berger, ed., (Weimar: Kiepenheuer: 1972), pp. 149f.

102 Cited in: Hildegard Meyer, *Nord-Amerika im Urteil des deutschen Schrifttums*, pp. 55-56.

103 Cited in: ibid., p. 56.

104 Rolf Engelsing, "Deutschland und die Vereinigten Staaten im 19. Jahrhundert," p. 145.

105 Hildegard Meyer, *Amerika im Urteil des deutschen Schrifttums*, p. 23.

106 On the literary concept of the "wild," see: Sigrid Weigel, *Topographien der Geschlechter. Kulturgeschichtliche Studien zur Literatur*, (Reinbek :Rowohlt, 1990), pp. 131ff.

107 Karlheinz Rossbacher, *Lederstrumpf in Deutschland*, (Munich: Fink, 1972), pp. 18ff.

108 Peter Uwe Hohendahl, "Von der Rothaut zum Edelmenschen. Karl Mays Amerikaromane," in: Sigrid Bauschinger, et al., *Amerika in der deutschen Literatur*, pp. 229-245.

NOTES FOR PAGES 29-51 (CONTINUED)

109 Jost Hermand, "Gralsmotive um die Jahrhundertwende," in: ——, *Von Mainz nach Weimar,* (Stuttgart: Metzler, 1969), p. 276.

110 Friedrich Nietzsche, *The Gay Science,* trans. Walter Kaufmann, (New York: Random House, 1974), chap. 329, pp. 258-59; German reprinted in: Ernst Fraenkel, *Amerika im Spiegel des deutschen politischen Denkens,* p. 301.

111 Günter Moltmann, "Deutscher Antiamerikanismus heute und früher," p. 95.

112 Karl Marx, *Marx-Engels Werke,* vol. 9, (Berlin: Dietz, 1963), p. 236.

113 Rolf Engelsing, "Deutschland und die Vereinigten Staaten im 19. Jahrhundert," p. 147.

114 Cited in: Ernst Fraenkel, *Amerika im Spiegel des deutschen politischen Denkens,* p. 28.

115 Carl Schurz, "Brief an Malwida v. Meysenbug," in: Malvida von Meysenbug, *Gesammelte Werke,* Stuttgart, Berlin, Leipzig 1922, vol. 1, pp. 310-313; reprint in: Ernst Fraenkel, *Amerika im Spiegel des deutschen politischen Denkens,* p. 158.

116 Wilhelm Liebknecht, *Ein Blick in die Neue Welt,* Stuttgart 1887, pp. 86-88, reprint in: Ernst Fraenkel, *Amerika im Spiegel des deutschen politischen Denkens,* p. 153.

117 Karl Kautsky, *Der amerikanische Arbeiter,* cited in: Ernst Fraenkel, ibid., p. 221.

118 Ulrich Ott, *Amerika ist anders,* p. 101.

119 Wilhelm von Polenz, *Das Land der Zukunft,* (Berlin:Fortuna, 1903), p. 402, cited in: Ulrich Ott, ibid., p. 108.

120 Gertrud Deicke, *Das Amerikabild in der deutschen öffentlichen Meinung von 1898-1914,* doctoral dissertation, Hamburg 1956, pp. 241ff.

121 Modris Eksteins, *Tanz über Gräber,* (Reinbek :Rowohlt,1989), p. 282.

122 Ibid., p. 124.

123 For a survey see Reinhard R. Doerries,"Empire and Republic: German-American Relations before 1917," in: Frank Trommler and McVeigh op.cit., pp. 3-17.

Notes for Pages 53-77

124 Adolf Halfeld, *Amerika und der Amerikanismus. Kritische Betrachtungen eines Deutschen und eines Europäers,* (Jena: Diederichs, 1927), p. X.

125 Ulrich Ott, *Amerika ist anders,* p. 164.

126 Peter Berg, *Deutschland und Amerika 1918-1929. Über das deutsche Amerikabild der zwanziger Jahre,* (Lübeck, Hamburg: Mathesen, 1963), p. 7.

127 Gesine Schwan, "Das deutsche Amerikabild seit derWeimarer Republik," p. 5.

128 See also Helmuth Plessner, *Die verspätete Nation. Über die politische Verfügbarkeit bürgerlichen Geistes,* (Stuttgart: Kohlhammer, 1959),

NOTES FOR PAGES 53-77 (CONTINUED)

2nd edition, pp. 44f.

129 Adolf Halfeld, *Amerika und der Amerikanismus*, p. 11.

130 Cited in: Ernst Fraenkel, "Das deutsche Wilsonbild," in: *Jahrbuch für Amerikastudien* 5 (1960), pp. 66-120, here: p. 109.

131 Adolf von Harnack, "Wilsons Botschaft an die deutsche Freiheit," in: *Die deutsche Freiheit* (5 speeches held on 18, 22, and 25 May 1917 in the Berlin House of Representatives), Gotha 1917, pp. 1-13, reprinted in: Ernst Fraenkel, *Amerika im Spiegel des deutschen politischen Denkens*, p. 241.

132 Cited in: Ernst Fraenkel, "Das deutsche Wilsonbild," p. 100.

133 Cited in: Ernst Fraenkel, ibid., p. 101.

134 *Deutsche Allgemeine Zeitung*, 14 May 1919, cited in: Peter Berg, *Deutschland und Amerika 1918-1929*, p. 24.

135 *Vorwärts*, 8 May 1919, cited in: Peter Berg, ibid., p. 24.

136 *Spartacusbrief* 12, October 1918, *Spartacusbriefe*, East Berlin 1958, p. 469, cited in: Peter Berg, ibid., p. 21.

137 *Rote Fahne*, 19 November 1918, cited in: Peter Berg, ibid., p. 20.

138 *Deutsche Zeitung*, 4 February 1924, cited in: Peter Berg, ibid., p. 45.

139 *Hilfe*, 15 May 1919, cited in: Peter Berg, ibid., p. 48.

140 *Preussische Jahrbücher*, vol. 188, pp. 23ff., cited in: Ernst Fraenkel, "Das deutsche Wilsonbild," p. 108.

141 Klaus Schwabe, "Anti-Americanism within the German Right 1917-1933," in: *Amerikastudien* 21/1 (1976), pp. 89-107, here: p. 102.

142 Ernst Fraenkel, "Das deutsche Wilsonbild," p. 119.

143 Klaus Schwabe, "Anti-Americanism within the German Right," p. 97.

144 Ibid., p. 96.

145 Ibid., p. 98.

146 Giselher Wirsing, *Der maßlose Kontinent. Roosevelts Kampf um die Weltherrschaft*, (Jena: Diederichs,1942), p. 229.

147 Reichsführer SS, "Amerikanismus—Eine Weltgefahr," n.p., n.d. (1944), p. 32.

148 Karl Haushofer, preface to Scott Nearing and Joseph Freeman, *Dollardiplomatie*, trans. Paul Fohr, Berlin 1927, p. V; English: Scott Nearing and Joseph Freeman, *Dollar Diplomacy*, (New York: Huebsch & Viking, 1925) repr. New York 1966.

149 Diary entry of 2 July 1918, reprinted in: Hans-Adolf Jacobsen, *Karl Haushofer. Leben und Werk*, 2 vols., (Boppard on the Rhine: Boldt, 1979), vol. 1, p. 153.

150 Clara Zetkin, speech before the Reichstag on 7 March 1923, *Protokolle* (proceedings), vol. 358, p. 991, cited in: Peter Berg, *Deutschland und Amerika 1918-1929*, pp. 82, 86. (The grammar of the speech excerpt is taken directly from the original transcription.)

151 Cited in: Alphons Silberner, *Kommunisten zur Judenfrage*, (Opladen: Westdeutscher Verlag, 1983), p. 268.

152 Alphons Silberner, *Sozialisten zur Judenfrage*, (Berlin: Colloquium,

NOTES FOR PAGES 53-77 (CONTINUED)

1962), pp. 206f.

153 Cited in: Peter Berg, *Deutschland und Amerika 1918-1929*, pp. 86, 93.

154 Giselher Wirsing, *Der maßlose Kontinent*, p. 188.

155 Arthur Salz, "Der Imperialismus der Vereinigten Staaten," in: *Archiv für Sozialwissenschaften und Sozialpolitik* 50 (1923), pp. 565-616, here: p. 547.

156 Charlotte Lütkens, "Die Amerikalegende," in: *Sozialistische Monatshefte* 38/1 (1932), pp. 45ff.

157 Klaus Schwabe, "Anti-Americanism within the German Right," pp. 96-97.

158 Adolf Halfeld, *Amerika und der Amerikanismus*, p. 38.

159 Ibid., p. 101.

160 Hermann Graf Keyserling, *Amerika. Der Aufgang einer neuen Welt*, (Stuttgart, Berlin: Deutsche Verlagsanstalt, 1930), p. 385.

161 Ibid., p. 305.

162 Ibid., pp. 378, 385.

163 Adolf Halfeld, *Amerika und der Amerikanismus*, p. 219.

164 Alfred Rosenberg, *Der Mythos des 20. Jahrhunderts*, Munich 1935, pp. 501f., cited in: Ernst Fraenkel, *Amerika im Spiegel des deutschen politischen Denkens*, p. 501.

165 Hermann Graf Keyserling, *Amerika*, p. 333.

166 C.G. Jung, "Die Erdbedingtheit der Psyche," lecture held at the conference of the School of Wisdom, "Der Leuchter," VIIIth yearbook of the Schule der Weisheit, Darmstadt 1927, reprinted in: Ernst Fraenkel, *Amerika im Spiegel des deutschen politischen Denkens*, p. 301.

167 Otto Bonhard, *Jüdische Weltherrschaft?*, Berlin 1928, p. 147, cited in: Klaus Schwabe, "Anti-Americanism within the German Right," p. 98.

168 Alexander Graf Brockdorff, *Amerikanische Weltherrschaft?*, (Berlin: Albrecht, 1929), p. 26.

169 Adolf Halfeld, *Amerika und der Amerikanismus*, p. 48.

170 Ibid., p. 239.

171 Alexander Graf Brockdorff, *Amerikanische Weltherrschaft?*, p. 11.

172 M. J. Bonn, *Geld und Geist. Vom Wesen und Werden der amerikanischen Welt*, (Berlin: S. Fischer, 1927), pp. 179ff.

173 Ulrich Ott, *Amerika ist anders*, p. 170.

174 Alfred Kerr, *Yankeeland—Eine Reise*, (Berlin: R. Moss,1925) p. 53.

175 Ulrich Ott, *Amerika ist anders*, p. 19.

176 Egon Erwin Kisch, "Paradies Amerika," vol. 4, *Gesammelte Werke*, (Berlin, Weimar: Aufbau, 1984), p. 215.

177 Thomas O. Brand, "Das Amerikabild Brechts," in: Alexander Ritter, ed., *Deutschlands literarisches Amerikabild*, pp. 451-467, here: p. 451.

178 Thomas O. Brand, "Das Amerikabild Brechts," p. 244; in contrast,

NOTES FOR PAGES 53-77 (CONTINUED)

cf. Marjorie L. Hoover, "'Ihr geht gemeinsam den Weg nach unten.' Aufstieg und Fall Amerikas im Werk Bertolt Brechts?," in: Sigrid Bauschinger, et al., *Amerika in der deutschen Literatur*, pp. 294-314. She criticizes Seliger's chronologization by seeing Brecht's critique of America as starting much earlier, p. 301.

179 Helfried W. Seliger, *Das Amerikabild Bertolt Brechts*, (Bonn: Bouvier, 1974), p. 177.

180 Thomas O. Brand, "Das Amerikabild Brechts," p. 462.

181 Ulrich Ott, *Amerika ist anders*, p. 204.

182 Egon Erwin Kisch, "Paradies Amerika," p. 143.

183 Hermann Graf Keyserling, *Amerika*, p. 378.

184 Adolf Halfeld, *Amerika und der Amerikanismus*, p. 49.

Notes for Pages 79-103

185 Otto Schäfer, *Imperium Americanum. Die Ausbreitung des Machtbereichs der Vereinigten Staaten*, (Essen; Essener Verlagsanstalt, 1943), p. 191.

186 James V. Compton, *The Swastika and the Eagle: Hitler, the United States, and the Origins of World War II*, (Boston: Houghton, Mifflin, 1967), p. 10.

187 Ibid., p. 14.

188 For a general outline see Detlef Junker," Roosevelt and the National Socialist Threat of the United States,"in: Frank Trommler and Joseph McVeigh op. cit., pp 30-44. James Compton, Hitler und die USA, op. cit. p.21.

189 Ibid., p. 17.

190 Adolf Hitler, *Mein Kampf*, (Munich: Eher, 1930), p. 723.

191 Hermann Rauschning, *Gespräche mit Hitler*, Zurich, Vienna 1940; reprinted in: Ernst Fraenkel, *Amerika im Spiegel des deutschen politischen Denkens*, p. 316; see also James V. Compton, *The Swastika and the Eagle*, p. 25.

192 Cited in: James V. Compton, *The Swastika and the Eagle*, p. 25.

193 Hans Dieter Schäfer, "Amerikanismus im Dritten Reich," in: Michael Prinz, Rainer Zitelmann, eds., *Nationalsozialismus und Modernisierung*, (Darmstadt: Wissenschaftliche Buchgesellschaft, 1991), pp. 199-215, here: pp. 203-205.

194 Hans Dieter Schäfer, "Das gespaltene Bewusstsein. Über die Lebenswirklichkeit in Deutschland 1933-1945," in : ———, *Das gespaltene Bewusstsein. Deutsche Kultur und Lebenswirklichkeit 1933-1945*, (Berlin: Ullstein, 1982), pp. 146-208, here: p. 164.

195 Harald Frisch, *Das deutsche Rooseveltbild 1933-1941*, doctoral dissertation, Berlin 1967, p. 101.

196 Saul Friedländer, *Auftakt zum Untergang. Hitler und die Vereinigten Staaten von Amerika 1939-1941*, Stuttgart, etc. 1965, pp. 18ff. transl. from *Prelude to Downfall: Hitler and the United States, 1939-41*, (New

NOTES FOR PAGES 79-103 (CONTINUED)

York: Knopf, 1967); Harald Frisch, *Das deutsche Rooseveltbild*, pp. 104ff.

197 Hans Dieter Schäfer, "Das gespaltene Bewusstsein," p. 170.

198 Ibid., pp. 175-176.

199 Reichsführer-SS, *Amerikanismus—eine Weltgefahr*, pp. 35-36. For a new and extensive study on this phenomenon, see Michael H. Kater, Different Drummers. Jazz in the Culture of Nazi Germany, (New York: Oxford University Press, 1992), pp.111 ff.

200 Hans Dieter Schäfer, "Amerikanismus im Dritten Reich," pp. 209, 214.

201 Ibid., p. 208.

202 Ibid., p. 215.

203 For example, Werner A. Lohe, *Roosevelt-Amerika*, Munich 1939, published by Verlag Franz Eher Nachf., GmbH; republished in 1942, with opening remarks of the Nazi Party, by their main press, Zentralverlag der NSDAP, as the successor publishers to Franz Eher.

204 Cited in: James V. Compton, *The Swastika and the Eagle*, p. 22.

205 Ibid., p. 21.

206 Max Domarus, *Hitler—Reden und Proklamationen 1932-1945*, with commentary by a contemporary, (Munich: Süddeutscher Verlag, 1965).

207 Cited in: Günter Moltmann, "Deutscher Anti-Amerikanismus heute und früher," p. 305.

208 Günter Moltmann, "Deutscher Anti-Amerikanismus heute und früher," p. 308.

209 Giselher Wirsing, *Der maßlose Kontinent*, p. 6.

210 Ibid., p. 176.

211 Ibid., pp. 188-189.

212 Ibid., pp. 186-187.

213 Ibid., pp. 189-190.

214 Ibid., pp. 190-191.

215 Ibid., p. 190.

216 Following the anti-Western international law tradition of the 1920s and 1930s, the journalist Günter Maschke tried to bring into position the entire stockpile of arguments typical of enemies of the "world" order of Weimar, Geneva, and Versailles, in the following article: Günter Maschke, "Frank B. Kellogg siegt am Golf. Völkerrechtsgeschichtliche Rückblicke anlässlich des ersten Krieges des Pazifismus," in: *Siebte Etappe*, Bonn, October 1991, pp. 28ff. Unless I am completely wrong, this stockpile still has a future. A key sentence from Maschke's updating of past references reads as follows: The war against Iraq did not serve the emergence of a 'New World Order' (Bush); instead, it prevented a truly new one. It served the distant prospect of an Arab unity, the potential emergence of an

NOTES FOR PAGES 79-103 (CONTINUED)

'international order for an extended area, with an intervention ban for powers foreign to that area.' The Arab world was and is as 'damaged by Versailles' as Germany, and that alone should make us stop and think about our politics." (p. 36) Günter Maschke sees himself as having been forced onto the fringes for years. He is wrong. Rather, he is not all that far from prevailing attitudes. His problem lies in the fact that the audience has not yet recognized that. But this is merely a question of time. See also the recent work: Rainer Zitelmann, Karlheinz Weissmann, Michael Grossheim, eds., *Westbindung. Chancen und Risiken für Deutschland*, (Berlin: Propyläen, 1993).

217 Giselher Wirsing, *Der maßlose Kontinent*, p. 188.
218 Adolf Halfeld, *USA greift in die Welt*, (Hamburg : Broschek, 1941), p. 141.
219 Ibid, p. 122.
220 Ibid, p. 147.
221 Ibid, pp. 58-59.
222 Ibid, p. 182.
223 Ibid, p. 183.
224 Ibid, p. 60.
225 Ibid, p. 176.
226 Cited in: Harald Frisch, *Das deutsche Rooseveltbild*, pp. 90-91.
227 Giselher Wirsing, *Der maßlose Kontinent*, p. 85.
228 Ibid., p. 99.
229 Ibid., p. 229.
230 Ibid., p. 150.
231 Ibid., p. 148.
232 Cited in: Hans-Jürgen Schröder, "Die amerikanische Exekutive in der Weltwirtschaftskrise: Roosevelts New Deal aus nationalsozialistischer Sicht," in: Raimund Borgmeier, Bernhard Reitz, *Zweihundert Jahre amerikanische Verfassung*, (Heidelberg: Winter, 1988), pp. 65-82, here: p. 73.
233 Cited in: Hans-Jürgen Schröder, "Die amerikanische Exekutive in der Weltwirtschaftskrise," p. 68.
234 Cited in: Harald Frisch, *Das deutsche Rooseveltbild*, p. 34.
235 Cited in: Hans-Jürgen Schröder, "Die amerikanische Exekutive in der Weltwirtschaftskrise," p. 69.
236 Cited in: Harald Frisch, *Das deutsche Rooseveltbild*, p. 45.
237 Cited in: Hans-Jürgen Schröder, "Die amerikanische Exekutive in der Weltwirtschaftskrise," p. 75.
238 Adolf Halfeld, *USA greift in die Welt*, p. 187.
239 *10 Jahre Adolf Hitler—10 Jahre Roosevelt*, Berlin 1943, p. 4.
240 Giselher Wirsing, *Der maßlose Kontinent*, p. 169.
241 Ibid., p. 166.
242 Ibid., p. 168.

NOTES FOR PAGES 79-103 (CONTINUED)

243 Ibid., p. 211.
244 Ibid., p. 434.
245 Ibid., p. 436.

Notes for Pages 105-150

246 Adolf Halfeld, *USA greift in die Welt*, (Hamburg: Broschek, 1942), p. 132.
247 Horst-Eberhard Richter, "Amerikanismus, Antiamerikanismus— oder was sonst?," in: *Psyche* 40 (1986), pp. 582-599, here: p. 583.
248 Ibid., p. 598.
249 Cited in: Günter Moltmann, "Deutscher Antiamerikanismus heute und früher," p. 309.
250 Cited in: Cedric Belfrage, *Seeds of Destruction*, New York, 1954, p. 1; Bernd Greiner, "Mit Sigmund Freud im Apfelhain—oder Was Deutsche in 45 Jahren über Henry Morgenthau gelernt haben," in: *Mittelweg* 35/3 (1992), pp. 44ff, here: p. 45.
250 Gabriela Wettberg, *Das Amerika-Bild und seine negativen Konstanten in der deutschen Nachkriegsliteratur*, (Heidelberg: Winter, 1987), p. 65.
252 Cited in: Bernd Greiner, "Mit Sigmund Freud im Apfelhain," p. 44.
253 Ibid., p. 50.
254 Ulrich Ott, *Amerika ist anders*, p. 356.
255 Norbert Muhlen, "German Anti-Americanism: East & West Zones. Clinical Notes for a Diagnosis—and Remedy," in: *Commentary* 15 (February 1953), pp. 121-130, here: p. 127. For a comprehensive outlook see Andrei S. Markovits, "Anti-Americanism and the Struggle for a West-German Identity" in: Peter H. Merkl (ed.), *The Federal Republic of Germany at Forty*, (New York: New York University Press, 1989) pp. 35-54.
256 Wolfgang Koeppen, *Tauben im Gras*, Stuttgart 1951, reprinted (Frankfurt: Suhrkamp 1980).
257 Ibid., p. 18.
258 Gabriela Wettberg, *Das Amerika-Bild und seine negativen Konstanten in der deutschen Nachkriegsliteratur*, p. 65.
259 Hans-Jürgen Grabbe, "Das Amerikabild Konrad Adenauers," in: *Amerikastudien* 31/3 (1986), pp. 315-323, here: p. 319.
260 Cited in: Jack Zipes, "Die Freiheit trägt Handschellen im Land der Freiheit. Das Bild der Vereinigten Staaten von Amerika in der Literatur der DDR," in: Sigrid Bauschinger, et al., *Amerika in der deutschen Literatur*, pp. 328-352, here: p. 328; on nationalism in the former GDR, see also: Sigrid Meuschel, *Legitimation und Parteiherrschaft in der DDR*, (Frankfurt/Main: Suhrkamp, 1992), pp. 101ff.
261 Norbert Muhlen, "German Anti-Americanism," p. 122.
262 Helfried W. Seliger, *Das Amerikabild des Bertolt Brechts*, (Bonn: Bouvier, 1974), p. 239, [Translation of the poem is my own—trans.]
263 Information from the Museum for City History in Dresden.

NOTES FOR PAGES 105-150 (CONTINUED)

264 Cited in: Wolfgang Wagner, "Das Amerikabild der Europäer," p. 22.
265 Rolf Winter, *Ami go home: Plädoyer für den Abschied von einem gewalt-tätigen Land,* (Hamburg : Rasch&Røohring, 1989), p. 11.
266 Ibid., p. 13.
267 Ibid., p. 23.
268 Ibid., p. 24.
269 Rolf Hochhuth, *Krieg und Klassenkrieg,* (Reinbek: Rowohlt,1971), p. 154.
270 Ibid., p. 153.
271 Ibid., p. 161.
272 Leo L. Matthias, *Die Kehrseite der USA,* (Reinbek: Rowohlt, 1964), p. 15.
273 Rolf Hochhuth, *Krieg und Klassenkrieg,* p. 156.
274 Caspar Schrenck-Notzing, *Charakterwäsche. Die amerikanische Be-satzung in Deutschland und ihre Folgen,* (Stuttgart: Seewald, 1965), p. 79.
275 Ibid., p. 182.
276 On the significance of the establishment of political science depart-ments in the Federal Republic of Germany, see Hans-Joachim Arndt, *Die Besiegten von 1945. Versuch einer Politologie für Deutsche samt Würdigung der Politikwissenschaft in der Bundesrepublik Deutsch-land,* (Berlin: Dunker & Humboldt, 1978).
277 Caspar Schrenck-Notzing,*Charakterwäsche,* p. 121.
278 Ibid., p. 123.
279 Ibid., p. 127.
280 Ibid., p. 231.
281 Ibid., p. 147f.; on the hiring policy in the political science depart-ments in the early phase of the Federal Republic, see Hans-Joachim Arndt, *Die Besiegten von 1945,* pp. 253ff.
282 Caspar Schrenck-Notzing, *Charakterwäsche,* p. 148.
283 Ibid., pp. 182-3.
284 Ibid., pp. 243-3.
285 For a general outline, see Anton Kaes ,"Mass Culture and Moder-nity: Notes Toward a Social History of early American and Ger-man Cinema," in Frank Trommler and Joseph McVeigh op. cit. pp. 317-331.
286 Manfred Henningsen, *Der Fall Amerika,* (München: List, 1974) p. 204.
287 In detail on the context of people and the literature genre, see: Ani-ta Krätzer, *Studien zum Amerikabild in der neueren deutschen Literatur, Max Frisch—Uwe Johnson—Hans Magnus Enzensberger und das "Kursbuch,"* Bern, Frankfurt/Main 1982, pp. 206ff.; affirmative: Klaus Peter, "Supermacht USA. Hans Magnus Enzensberger über Amerika, Politik und Verbrechen," in: Sigrid Bauschinger, et al., *Amerika in der deutschen Literatur,* pp. 368-381. For a convincing sur-

NOTES FOR PAGES 105-150 (CONTINUED)

vey of anti-American trends in this literature, see: Manfred Durzak, "Abrechnung mit einer Utopie? Das Amerika-Bild im jüngsten deutschen Roman," in: ———, *Das Amerika-Bild in der deutschen Gegenwartsliteratur*, pp. 172-200.

288 Hans Magnus Enzensberger, "Reflexionen vor einem Glaskasten," in: ———, *Politik und Verbrechen*, (Frankfurt/Main: Suhrkamp, 1964), p. 25.

289 Hans Magnus Enzensberger, "Über die Schwierigkeiten, ein Inländer zu sein," in: ———, *Deutschland, Deutschland unter anderem. Äußerungen zur Politik*, Frankfurt/Main: Suhrkamp, 1968), p. 12.

290 Hans Magnus Enzensberger, "Reflexionen vor einem Glaskasten," pp. 26f. See also: Exchange of letters, Hannah Arendt and H.M. Enzensberger, reprinted in the Merkur April 1965, pp. 380-385.

291 Heiner Kipphardt, "Bruder Eichmann. Protokolle, Materialien," in: *Kursbuch* 51 (1978), pp. 17-41.

292 Reinhard Lettau, "Dossier 1: Täglicher Faschismus. Evidenz aus fünf Monaten," in: *Kursbuch* 22/1970, pp. 1-44.

293 Ibid., p. 8.

294 Hans Magnus Enzensberger, *Das Verhör in Havanna*, (Frankfurt/Main: Suhrkamp 1972 [1970]), p. 4.

295 Matthias Dienstag, "Trauer um Nixon," in *Kursbuch* 37 (1974), p. 184. Such a perspective was also promoted by prominent philosophers. For example, Ernst Bloch expressed such a traditional view, in "Die neue Linke und die Tradition," in: *Abschied von der Utopie?*, Frankfurt/Main 1980, pp. 155ff, pp. 160-61. His comments on America were disparaging and anti-mercantile: "This way of thinking comes from the business sector . . . . It is a businesslike, pragmatic position that is greatly fostered by America and the influence of America.—But what is that of our business?"

296 Cited in: Klaus Peter, *Supermacht USA*, p. 357.

297 Anita Krätzer, *Studien zum Amerikabild in der neueren deutschen Literatur*, p. 187.

298 Gabriela Wettberg, *Das Amerika-Bild und seine negativen Konstanten in der deutschen Nachkriegsliteratur*, p. 9.

299 Uwe Johnson, *Jahrestage. Aus dem Leben der Gesine Cresspahl*, vol. 1, (Frankfurt/Main: Suhrkamp, 1972 [1970]), p. 21.

300 Rolf Winter, *Ami go home*, p. 131. On the significance of the genocide of the Native Americans as a stigma, see: Günter C. Behrmann, "Geschichte und aktuelle Struktur des Antiamerikanismus," in: *Aus Politik und Zeitgeschichte*, vols. 29, 30 (1984), pp. 3-14, here: p. 7: "In a presentation of American politics exhibiting typical modern anti-Americanism, the fate of the Indians is shown as representing the beginning of a development with an apparently inner consistency leading to the 'final scene,' to America's 'final battle,' to the planning of a nuclear 'first strike' against the Soviet

NOTES FOR PAGES 105-150 (CONTINUED)

Union."

301 Cf. also André Glucksman, *La Force du Vertige*, (Paris: Grasset 1983), pp. 127f.

302 Ernst von Salomon, *Der Fragebogen*, (Hamburg: Rowohlt, 1951), p. 614.

303 Detlef Hartmann, "Völkermord gegen soziale Revolution," in: *Autonomie*, n.s., 1985, pp. 217ff.

304 Ibid., p. 221.

305 Ibid., p. 238.

306 Reinhard Opitz, *Faschismus und Neofaschismus*, (Frankfurt/Main: Marxistische Blätter, 1988), p. 224.

307 Detlef Hartmann, "Völkermord gegen soziale Revolution," p. 243.

308 Ibid., p. 243.

309 For an example, published by a Social Democratic Party publishers, see: Jürgen Bruhn, *Schlachtfeld Europa oder Amerikas letztes Gefecht. Gewalt und Wirtschaftsimperialismus in der US-Aussenpolitik seit 1840*, (Bonn: Dietz, 1983).

310 All quotations cited in: Arnulf Baring, *Unser neuer Grössenwahn. Deutschland zwischen Ost und West*, (Stuttgart: Deutsche Verlagsanstalt, 1988), pp. 129-30, 136.

311 Rolf Winter, *Ami go home*, pp. 32, 35.

312 Alfred Mechtersheimer, "Antiamerikanisch—weshalb eigentlich nicht? Von der Pflicht, dem weltweit verheerenden Einfluss der USA zu widerstehen," in: Helmut Thielen, ed., *Der Krieg der Köpfe. Vom Golfkrieg zur neuen Weltordnung*, (Bad Honnef, Horlemann, 1991).

313 Ibid., p. 105.

314 Ibid., p. 108.

315 Ibid., p. 108.

316 Ibid., p. 115.

317 Anton Zischka, *Ölkrieg*, (Leipzig : Goldmann, 1939).

318 Ibid., pp. 145ff.

319 Alfred Mechtersheimer, "Antiamerikanisch—weshalb eigentlich nicht?" p. 114.

320 Rolf Winter, *Ami go home*, p. 326.

321 Ibid., p. 192.

322 Ibid., p. 335.

323 Asmus Petersen, "Fire and Forget," in: *Kursbuch* 105 (1991), pp. 59-70, here: 61-62.

324 Ibid., p. 67.

325 Max Horkheimer, *Kritische Theorie*, vol. 1, (Frankfurt/Main: Suhrkamp, 1968), p. XIII.

Index

Photo Credits